MW01165250

When The Unlikely Are Chosen

Dear Sister Vera Kennedy,
You are an inspiration.
Hope you enjoy my journey
of grace and gratitude.
Love
Judge Kathryn J. Lewis
1/25/2020

When The Unlikely Are Chosen

Kathryn Streeter Lewis

Printed in the United States of America.

For information on special pricing for bulk orders or requests for permission to reproduce any portion of this book must be emailed to:

judgekslewis@gmail.com

All photos courtesy of author's collection unless otherwise noted. About the Author photo by photographer Richard Quindry.

Some of the names in this book have been changed.

ISBN: 9781700093905

DEDICATION

The Power of Dad

John D. Streeter
(1924 - 2000)

There is a place that most people rarely think about, the heart of a black man, born poor but determined to make a better life for his children than he had the opportunity to achieve. What he couldn't give them in material things he made up for with something so much more valuable: his presence. Not a "yeah, I'm here, what else do you want" presence but a presence that understands that you don't just talk about character, courage, respect, responsibility, discipline, education and love. You live it.

Dads who accept, with pride, the mantle of fatherhood don't make the cover of popular magazines for this significant accomplishment. They are often remembered but seldom memorialized. This book honors fathers who deserve their due. Why do I care? Because for too long, society has been misinformed about the contributions and successes of unsung fathers who, against all odds, sent forth into the world, girls imbued with strength and character instilled in them by their fathers. Too often the prevailing image of a poor black man as a father figure is less than positive. He is more often portrayed as absent, disinterested, lacking whatever it takes to develop children who will become productive adults.

As the old folks used to say, "It's time the truth be told." It is time to correct the record and share with others the father who made the difference in my life. Fathers like him made a difference in the lives of many. He is not an anomaly. There is another image of fathers that lives in the hearts of their children. In these pages, I reflect on the lessons my father taught me and how I used them. I pay tribute to my father and fathers like him who have been overlooked or distorted in the portrait of what makes a good father. More than invaluable lessons, my father John D. Streeter, by his example, taught me to revere the power of a dad.

CONTENTS

FOREWORD

When my mother first told me about her desire to write a memoir, I was immediately supportive. As she started to write and share excerpts of the book, I was able to revisit a series of stories my mother used to recount over the years. These stories would be shared almost like parables when certain situations would arise, like when I wanted to react out of emotion because someone wronged me. In addition to the stories, my mother also had a plethora of old sayings that accompanied these stories. These sayings almost exclusively seemed to be passed down from my grandfather.

I was fortunate to have my grandfather in my life throughout my childhood, and even when his health declined, his mind was still sharp up until his death. I am not surprised that my grandfather plays such a pivotal role in her memoir. After reading the completed memoir, my view of my grandfather evolved. I always thought he was a man of great intellect and character who was extremely intentional about how he lived his life and raised his children. I thought this based on the myriad of stories and sayings that my mother shared with me, in addition to just being around my grandfather as a child.

How my mother reconstructed her upbringing in this memoir, actually painted a picture of my grandfather as an iconoclast. I did not think this prior to reading the book, but my grandfather fought tooth and nail against institutionalized racism and sexism to make sure his daughter obtained a quality education. He did this despite being a chauvinist, as my mother notes in the book. Being invisible to many in authority is a through line in this memoir. My grandfather did not just make my mother feel seen, but he made sure that others in positions of authority saw her. We now live in a world where "allyship" is often discussed in the context of striving for equality based on gender, race, sexual orientation, and gender identity. My grandfather showed that true allyship doesn't come just from seeing someone for what they have to offer, but making sure others see the value in others too.

This memoir also made me think about my own upbringing and how it was influenced by my mother's childhood and early life. My mother also made me feel seen, but she also made sure I felt seen in a positive light; because all too often, black boys were, and are, either not seen or not seen in a positive light. And for a little boy who was often in situations, especially at school, where he was the only or one of just a few black boys, my mother, like her father, *made my dream her fight*. And while "fight" sounds a bit heavy-handed, in the '50s and '60s when my mother was growing up, it required a figurative fight to get a black girl the opportunities she deserved. But even in the '80s and '90s when I was growing up, it still took a fight—even when you and your husband are paying expensive private school and private university tuition. One would think that the fight would end once my mother attained some level of professional and economic success, but the fight still continued, and she was well equipped after seeing the example of her father. When I become a father, my expectation is that I will have to fight too because my professional and economic success will not negate some of the realities that still exist in society today for black and brown people.

This memoir serves not only as a story of *when* the unlikely are chosen but *how* someone so unlikely can succeed.

Michael Streeter Lewis
October 12, 2019

Introduction: All Rise

July 15, 1988: Worlds collided in this room. Everyone was here by choice and glad to witness this event.

Mom and Dad held my judicial robe as my son, Michael, age seven, stood in front of me to fasten it. My husband, Michael, stood behind me as our son held the Bible upon which I placed my hand and took the oath of office. I had been appointed by Governor Robert P. Casey, confirmed by the Pennsylvania Senate, and now it was official. I was a judge of the Commonwealth of Pennsylvania Court of Common Pleas for the First Judicial District in Philadelphia, Pennsylvania. Judge Edward Bradley, the president judge, had unofficially sworn me in two weeks prior to this ceremony so that I could begin hearing cases after my appointment was confirmed. Now, before a standing-room audience in the ceremonial courtroom, he invited me to come and take a seat on the bench with the judges who were presiding at my public swearing-in ceremony. I walked up the steps to the applause of the crowd and took my seat. The serious look on my face masked my desire to jump up and down. An indescribable awe filled me from head to toe. Is this really happening to me? Who would have thought that the path for a little black girl from a public housing project in North Philadelphia would lead to being sworn in as a judge? The thunderous applause and shouts filled the sun-drenched, ornate courtroom in City Hall.

I took my seat and before any words escaped my mouth, I seized a once-in-a-lifetime opportunity. I looked into the faces of as many people in that room as I could before my silence became too awkward, and remembered when our lives intersected. Seated on the bench to my far left was the Honorable A. Leon Higginbotham, Jr., United States Court of Appeals for the Third Circuit. He was my mentor and friend. I met him when I was 15 years old, a sophomore in high school. Next to him was Justice Juanita Kidd Stout, the first African American woman to sit on the Pennsylvania Supreme Court. It was an honor to be appointed to fill her vacancy on the Court of Common Pleas. She was the first African American woman elected to the Philadelphia Court of Common Pleas. Seated next to her was Judge Nicholas Cipriani, administrative judge of the Family Court Division where I was assigned. I first met Judge Cipriani when I served as a law clerk for Judge Doris May Harris, my first job after law school. They shared chambers. His presence here reminded me of Judge Harris, the first African American woman judge I had ever met, and how fortunate I was that she picked me to be her law clerk. Judicial clerkships were highly coveted. Judge Harris and I kept in touch until her death in April 1985.

I looked at my family seated in the jury box. Those who were not designated a seat in the jury box arrived early to ensure that they got a seat as close to the front of the courtroom as possible. They all had a look of pride and astonishment. I focused my gaze on Dad, Michael, and Mom. They looked so serious, proud and ready to always be there for me. Their strength brought me to this day. The sacrifices they made to get me here were beyond measure.

The only person in the jury box who was not related to me was my fourth-grade teacher, Mrs. Epsie Holmes. She was retired now. I made a special effort to find her and ask her to be here and sit with my family. In the fourth grade, she bestowed on me a simple act of kindness. She combed my hair when I came to school near tears because no one combed it when my mother went to the hospital early to give birth to my sister Marilyn. That simple act of kindness instilled in me a lesson that I would never forget. She taught me that in order to make a positive difference in someone's life, I had to be willing to reach beyond my job description. Her face was aglow as she smiled at me just as she did when I was in the fourth grade. She represented the teachers and counselors who had such a profound impact on my life. I wished that my high school principal, Dr. Marcus A. Foster, was here. But he was killed by the Symbionese Liberation Army (SLA) in Oakland, California in 1973.

I continued to look around the room. There was the mayor, federal and state judges, members of city council, state senators and representatives, ministers, bar association leaders, government officials, friends from every stage of my life, my sisters from Alpha Kappa Alpha Sorority, Inc., present and former co-workers, including attorneys, secretaries, paralegals, clerks, messengers, neighbors from the 2600 block of North 30th Street where I grew up, members from the church that I attended as a child and my current church family. There were so many people I could only catch a brief glimpse of all the faces in the room. I couldn't remember an event where so many people from so many different backgrounds and experiences came together. At the beginning of the ceremony, many of the recognized dignitaries and clergy made remarks and extended well wishes.

Now, it was my turn to speak. I was glad that I seized the time to step outside of myself to take in what was happening in that room and inside of me. I was put on a road that led here when I was six years old. I never dreamed that this day was planned for me.

The room was filled with family, friends, teachers, mentors, and sponsors who taught me many lessons and guided me through an uncharted course. They were the dream carriers and conductors on the Underground Railroad that transported me to this place.

PART I

STREETERISMS

1

A Chauvinist Breaks Down Doors Closed to His Daughter's Dream

My curiosity about the law was ignited when four white men jumped out of a car and broke down our next-door neighbor's front door. The car screeched to a halt in front of our house, and the men ran onto Mr. Bumper's porch. The first man up the steps pounded hard on Mr. Bumper's door with his fist. I was six years old. I went to the black wrought-iron railing that separated our porches.

"Mr. Bumper is in a wheelchair. He can't come to the door real fast," I said.

The men did not look in my direction, tell me to stand back, or acknowledge that I was even there. I didn't know it at the time, but this would be the first of many times that someone would treat me as if I were invisible. Even at six years old, it didn't feel right.

When Mr. Bumper didn't come to the door, one of the men shouted, "Take the door!"

No sooner than the command was given, a short, fat white man with a long, round iron pole rammed Mr. Bumper's door. The force of the blow broke the lock that held two glass front-door panels together. Glass flew everywhere, onto the porch and into Mr. Bumper's vestibule. I took a deep breath but couldn't move. When one of the door panels fell from its hinges, the men ran inside. I clung to the railing with all my might. I could hear and feel my heart thumping. Mom and Dad came running out of our house onto the porch. Dad quickly pulled me away from the railing.

Until that moment, it had been a good day. It was a sunny afternoon in the summer of 1958. I was rocking in one of the three red rocking chairs on our front porch. The front door was open but the screen door was closed. Mom and Dad were in the living room talking and the TV was on. We lived in a predominantly black, working-class neighborhood in the Strawberry Mansion section of North Philadelphia. Fifty-two two-story row houses lined the 2600 block of North 30th Street; a delicatessen, hardware store, small grocery store, and an appliance store were the anchor businesses on each corner. None were owned by anyone who looked like those who lived in the neighborhood.

Four white men, not wearing uniforms, jumping quickly out of a car, attracted everyone's attention. Neighbors gathered and whispered to each other. "What's goin' on? Is that the cops?" Others stood silent and just watched.

By this time, I was running around, as Mom described it, like a chicken with its head cut off, asking questions. "Why? Can they do that?"

Someone grabbed me, made me keep still, and said, "Be quiet, girl, that's the law."

That event, the matter-of-fact non-explanation given to me at the time, and my unrelenting curiosity ignited my desire to become a lawyer. The seed was planted. In the late 1950s I was not old enough to understand the civil rights battles that raged throughout the United States. "Separate but equal" had been declared illegal by the United States Supreme Court in a series of decisions including Brown vs. Board of Education of Topeka, Kansas in 1954. The path from the ghetto to become a lawyer was a well-kept secret, if it existed at all for little black girls. It was highly unlikely that my dream to become a lawyer would be achieved.

* * *

As I got older, it seemed to me that the law had something to do with everything. I was amazed at how far the law reached into everybody's life. I showed Mom the tag on my bed pillow that read *Do not remove under penalty of law*. I was sure that I wanted to be a lawyer.

When I was in elementary school, Dad asked me, "What do you want to be when you grow up?"

Dad always asked me, my brother, and my sisters this question. This time, without hesitation or my usual list of choices, I said, "I want to be a lawyer."

"You want to be lawyer?"

I could tell he was surprised. He studied me as I did my homework at the dining room table. I often wondered what Dad thought when I told him my career choice. He was an unabashed male chauvinist who believed it was the natural order of things for men to lead and be in charge of everything. Women, even smart women, were to take care of the home and the children.

In the early 1960s, I doubt if Dad knew any women lawyers, black or white, personally or by reputation. Law was a profession for men, chauvinist men just like him. Dad was politically and socially astute. He knew that chauvinism was not to be confused with the more pernicious sexism which was also prevalent in society. Most seats of power, at least in government, were held by lawyers who were white men. Dad knew that it would be very difficult for me to become a lawyer. Sexism presented a hurdle but the pervasive, malignant cancer of racism presented a mountain. I would have to confront and get over both if my dream was ever to be realized. The Civil Rights Movement was heating up and constantly in the news. Times were changing but not without a fight.

Dad didn't express any of these thoughts when I told him

that I wanted to be a lawyer. Instead he said, "You can be anything you want to be if you're willing to work for it. Find out what you got to do to become a lawyer. How long you got to go to school for that? Look into that and get back to me. We'll talk about it."

I asked my teachers and anyone else who I thought might know what I had to do to become a lawyer. When I told my friends that I wanted to be a lawyer and what I had to do, many of them said, "Shucks, that's too much school. If you don't pass that Bar Exam test, you still won't be a lawyer. Don't know why you want to go through all that. But you go right ahead."

My friends were not trying to discourage me or be mean out of jealousy or any malicious intent. They understood reality as it played out where we lived, all around us every day. Nobody who lived on our block had gone to college, and most of our parents had not graduated from high school. Most of my friends had two parents living at home. The men worked full time; some had to work more than one job to earn as much as one full-time job. Most of the women on the block worked for minimum wage; a few worked full-time, many worked part-time or did "days-work" (a private home domestic worker) a couple of days a week. For girls, a good outcome was to graduate from high school on time without any children, not pregnant, and employable. My parents were no exception; neither of them graduated from high school. Dad worked full-time as a security guard for the City of Philadelphia, which was considered a good job. Against Dad's wishes, Mom worked part-time in housekeeping for the Board of Education at the elementary school around the corner. Before that, she worked part-time at the corner delicatessen and did days-work on the weekends. Mom and Dad understood the realities of that time, especially what was needed to survive in the marginalized space that defined the boundaries of our world. That's why they placed a high premium on education. They made sure that all of their children went to school every day, on time, and did what was expected. The status quo distorted and, in many cases, totally obliterated many of my friends' visions of what they could achieve in the future.

When I told Dad what I found out about what I had to do to become a lawyer, he said, "If you study hard, you can be a lawyer and I'm with you."

If I was going to become a lawyer, I had a lot to learn. I told Dad about the educational requirements and the Bar Exam. But he didn't tell me something that, in hindsight, I understand he already knew. The most important lessons that I needed to learn would be taught outside the classroom from an unwritten curriculum.

* * *

After elementary school I was sent to a junior high school outside of my neighborhood. It was located in a predominantly white and Jewish section of the city. Most of the students who attended the school lived in that neighborhood. I had to take the bus and the subway to get to school; it took 45 minutes each way. My neighborhood junior high school was located just a short 10-minute walk from my house. Dad and my elementary school teachers agreed that I should not go there because the school outside of my neighborhood was considered academically superior.

Civil rights marches and sit-ins were continuing in the South. I made a scrapbook with pictures I cut out of *Ebony* magazine. The pictures showed dogs attacking civil rights marchers as they ran from the police. I watched on television as black people were pushed to the ground by the force of fire hoses turned on them by the police. In March of 1963, the March on Washington was on the news, and everyone in the neighborhood was talking about it. Dad took off from work and went to the March on Washington. That was a few months before I graduated from elementary school.

I never traveled outside the neighborhood without Mom or Dad, and I was anxious about going to a school far away from home by myself. Most of my friends went to the neighborhood junior high school. When I asked Dad why couldn't I go to junior high school with my friends, he said, "If you want to be lawyer, you gotta keep your mind on your school work."

Looking back, I wonder if Dad wanted to reconsider his decision to send me out of the neighborhood to school after four black girls, who were about my age, were killed when their church was bombed on September 15, 1963 in Birmingham, Alabama. I had been at my new school less than two weeks.

I missed not going to junior high school with the friends I grew up with. They told me about the dances on the roof of the school at lunchtime and all the neighborhood drama that played out in school during the day. But I made new friends. Most of them were transferred to this school because their parents didn't want them to go to their neighborhood schools. I spent time with my old friends after school and on weekends.

In eighth grade, students were required to select the course curriculum they wanted to take in the ninth grade. Course curriculums included general studies, trade preparatory, commercial, commercial academic, and academic. I knew that if I wanted to go to college, I had to take the academic curriculum or commercial academic. I didn't want to take commercial academic because I would have to take typing. Between seventh and eighth grades, I signed up to take typing in summer school. After the teacher, Mrs. Lovett, cracked my knuckles with a wooden ruler because I didn't keep my wrists up, I decided that typing wasn't for me. When the day came to make my selection, I signed up for the academic curriculum.

Later that day, my homeroom teacher told me to go to Mr. Saltz's office. He was the career guidance counselor. When I got there, my curriculum selection form was on his desk. He smiled and asked me to sit down. Next, he asked if I knew that I had to take a foreign language and algebra if I took the academic curriculum.

"Yes," I said.

He kept smiling. "What do you want to be when you grow up?"

I proudly told him what I told everyone who asked me that. "I am going to be a lawyer."

He looked stunned, leaned back in his chair, cleared his throat, and now he smiled nervously.

"Kathy, you do such nice things with your hair, perhaps you should consider becoming a cosmetologist, and for that you should take trade preparatory. You might consider the commercial curriculum if you think you would like to be a secretary and work in a nice office someday. Think about it and let me know tomorrow."

I quietly left his office. It felt as if I had been punched in the stomach. I thought, Mr. Saltz was the guidance counselor and he knew more about this stuff than I did. I hung my head, got my books from the locker, and met my friends to go home. No one had ever told me that I couldn't be a lawyer.

As usual that evening my family gathered for dinner around the kitchen table. We always ate dinner together, except when Dad worked the 3 p.m. to 11 p.m. shift. Dad sat at one end of the table and Mom at the other end. Dad started the dinner conversation by asking my older brother, Johnny, "What did you do in school today? Have you finished your homework?"

This was how the conversation around the dinner table always started. Johnny and I knew the answers to these questions better be right. This was not idle chatter. Dad listened not only to what we said but how we said it. He looked in our eyes when he spoke to us, and we were taught to look people in the eye when they spoke to us and to keep our heads and voices up when we answered.

When it came my turn, I told Dad that the eighth graders selected their course curriculum for the ninth grade today and that I chose the academic curriculum. Then I told him what Mr. Saltz said about my hair, that I should be a cosmetologist and take the trade preparatory curriculum. Dad stopped eating, his fork poised midway between the plate and his mouth. He frowned as he looked at my hair. In the sixth grade I had won a long, hard-fought battle with Mom to do my own hair. That morning I was not able to decide which of four hairstyles to wear: a flip, a pageboy, bun atop my head, or a French roll. So, I wore all four together to school that day. The extent of my hairstyling ability was obvious. Dad frowned as he stared at my hair.

"Did you wear your hair like that to school today?"

"Yes, what's wrong with it?" I asked defensively. He didn't answer.

"Tell me again what that counselor told you about the course you should take next year."

I repeated what Mr. Saltz said.

"I thought you wanted to be a lawyer?"

I sighed. "Well, yeah, I do, but he said—"

Dad stopped eating, dropped his fork on his plate, and interrupted me. "Don't you have to take that college preparatory or that academic course to go to college?"

"Yes." I squirmed in my seat. Was I in trouble? Had I done something wrong? Everyone could see that Dad was angry. A hush invaded the room and everyone sat still.

Dad bit his bottom lip hard, his nostrils flared, and he looked straight ahead at Mom. In a voice that exhibited controlled anger he said, "Margaret, do I have a clean white shirt in the closet? Please get it ready for me. I will be up to that school first thing in the morning." Then he turned to me, his tone stern, cool, and tinged with anger, and said, "You're going to college and you're going to take that college preparatory course next year. Now if they try and stop you, I'll be down to the Board of Education. I am going to get me some answers."

Again, Dad focused his attention on my exotic array of hairstyles and shook his head in disbelief. We finished dinner in silence. Dad's disgust hung in the air like an ominous storm cloud waiting to burst.

After dinner, Johnny and I huddled around the dining room table and finished our homework. We whispered about what we thought Dad was going to do when he went to school tomorrow. We didn't know but our imaginations ran wild.

I got up earlier than usual the next morning and asked Dad if I was going with him to school. Dad looked in the mirror as he put his tie on and said, "No, you go to school just as you always do. Don't worry. Everything is going to be all right."

He didn't sound angry anymore, but I could tell he was trying to put me at ease. I watched him put his tie on. It was as if he was strapping on a weapon, preparing to go to war.

I arrived at school that morning and went to my homeroom. On the way to my first period class, I walked past the counselors' office and saw Dad in Mr. Saltz's office. From the hallway I couldn't hear anything, but Dad was leaning on Mr. Saltz's desk. His eyes were dark, no smile on his face, and he was pointing his finger at Mr. Saltz and around the room at the other two white people sitting in the office. I quickly walked away. I knew that if Dad wanted me there, he would have brought me along. I didn't want him to catch me peeping in.

After lunch, I was told to report to the counselors' office. Mr. Saltz was waiting for me. He was not smiling and his face turned red when I came in the office. He pushed the curriculum selection form across his desk and told me to sign it at the bottom. I was in the academic curriculum for ninth grade. I wanted to jump up and down, laugh, and clap my hands. But I didn't show any emotion, just signed the form. "You're excused." He took the form, turned his back to me, placed it in a file cabinet behind his desk, and slammed the drawer.

When I got home from school, Dad was sitting in the living room reading the newspaper. I asked, "What happened this morning?"

He knew I wanted all the details, but he wasn't going to report what went on to me. "Did you sign up for your course for next year?"

"Yes, and Mr. Saltz didn't compliment me on my hair today."

I told him what happened when I saw Mr. Saltz. With a grunt, Dad just smirked.

"You know you got to study hard. You're going to be a lawyer someday, and don't you let anybody tell you otherwise. Now give me a hug and get out of here. I want to finish reading my newspaper."

There would be other encounters at school when Dad showed up to investigate and demand that I be treated fairly. Even though I got into the academic curriculum, there were more battles ahead. Some teachers were fine and I didn't sense any different treatment. For example, Mrs. Shore taught French, which was not spoken by anyone in my neighborhood. She was an excellent teacher who made learning fun. I felt welcomed in her class, and there was an expectation that I could and would learn to speak French. However, the same could not be said for all the teachers at this school. There came a time when I encountered an openly hostile attitude from one of my teachers that caused me to go to Dad to protect my back and level the playing field.

It was mid-April 1966. I was in history class. The desk and chairs were connected and bolted to the floor. I was assigned the next-to-the-last seat on the last row in the classroom. There were approximately 33 students in my ninth-grade history class. Mr. Tyler gave a history test, and after the test he told us to exchange papers with the person sitting next to us. It was expected that we would mark each other's test paper. This was nothing new. We marked each other's test papers before in Mr. Tyler's and other classes. Mr. Tyler stood in front of the class reading answers to the test questions. Beth leaned over and asked me about a word on my paper. Beth sat next to me in class, and we had exchanged test papers. I answered her question. Then Beth and I looked in Mr. Tyler's direction. He had stopped talking and was looking at us. He tilted his head slightly to one side and said, "Now if you're so interested in what you got on this test, let me show you, so that you and everyone else will know."

He appeared to be speaking to Beth and me. He raised his voice and demanded that Beth give him my test paper. He stared at me as he tore my paper into pieces and balled them up in his fist. The class became eerily silent. A few students glanced quickly back at me, and Mr. Tyler brusquely told them, "Turn around, turn around." He kept his eyes on me even as he spoke to the class.

Until that moment it had been a good day. It was a couple days after my 14th birthday. I was wearing the birthday present that Mom and Dad bought for me, a new navy-blue trench coat. I had never been in trouble in school before. I was the quick-witted kid who kept other kids laughing, and the teacher could count on me to participate in class. Now here I was, half-sitting on one knee in my seat, the object of Mr. Tyler's ire and embarrassed in front of the class. That test grade was important because it was near the end of the semester, and I wanted to get a good grade in Mr. Tyler's class. I felt my chest tighten. I stared at Mr. Tyler as he glared at me. His displeasure was unmistakable. I felt tears welling in my eyes. But there was no way that I was going to let Mr. Tyler make me cry in front of the class. My mother used to say to me when she asked me to do something I didn't want to do, "If eyes could talk, young lady, I know what you would be saying." Well, I hoped my look spoke the anger and hate I felt for Mr. Tyler at that moment.

We stared at each other for a few moments, though it felt a lot longer. Then Mr. Tyler said, "Now sit all the way down in your seat and take off that raincoat."

He rolled his eyes and turned his back to me. I plopped down in my seat.

"It's not a raincoat, it's an all-weather coat," I said softly but loud enough to be heard. My tone was surly.

Mr. Tyler pivoted quickly around to face me. His face was red and his mouth was open in the shape of an "O." He was astounded, sheer disbelief that I dared to talk back to him. Sneering, he said, "So what? What's the difference between a raincoat and an all-weather coat?"

I quickly retorted, "It doesn't rain in all-weather, does it?"

A few snickers escaped a few of my once silent classmates. Mr. Tyler's face became a deeper red. His anger unleashed, he shouted, "You get out of here! Go to the principal's office right now." He thrust his arm out and pointed his finger at the door.

I gathered my stuff quickly, looking directly at him as I left the room. "I'm going to tell my father how you treated me."

Now Mr. Tyler was totally unhinged. He yelled, "Get out, get out! Tell anybody you want."

The bell for the next period rang. I went immediately to the principal's office, and I told the vice principal everything that happened in Mr. Tyler's class. I explained that Mr. Tyler was wrong for tearing up my paper and that he only did that to keep me from getting a good grade in his class. My test grades up to that time were A's and B's. The vice principal sent me to the counselor's office. She called Mr. Tyler on the telephone and told him that I was in her office. I could not hear what he said. She hung the phone up and told me that if I apologized to Mr. Tyler, I could go back to his class tomorrow. I couldn't believe what she said. I looked at her and thought, *Didn't any of you hear me?* Again, I felt invisible. My thoughts and feelings didn't count for anything. They didn't matter.

The bell rang. Last period ended. It was time to go home. The counselor asked, "Before you leave, do you want to go and apologize to Mr. Tyler so you can get back in his class tomorrow?"

At that moment all I really wanted to do was cry and start throwing stuff. But I didn't do either.

"I want talk to my father. Can I go now?"

"Yes, you can go, but Kathy, you will have to apologize to Mr. Tyler before he will let you back in his class."

Dad was not home from work when I got there. My brother, Johnny, was in the living room watching television, and I told him what happened in school.

"You better tell Dad as soon as he gets here. You lucky your butt didn't get suspended."

"Suspended for what? I didn't do nothing! If he thought we were cheating on the test, why didn't he tear up Beth's paper too? He just doesn't like me, and he wants to find a way to flunk me," I screamed and paced back and forth.

At that moment the front door opened and Dad came in. He always had a serious look on his face. I am sure he heard me screaming at Johnny from outside.

"Hey, how y'all doin'? What's all this arguing about?"

"Kathy, you better tell him. Are you going to tell him now?"

Dad unbuckled his gun holster and took off his black tie. This was all part of his Philadelphia Water Department security guard uniform. Now he was curious. "Tell me what?"

He looked from Johnny to me. Suddenly I blurted out the whole story nonstop, without taking a breath from beginning to end. By the time I reached the end of the story, I was crying and getting angrier each time I told it. Dad stood still and strained to take in what I was saying as I ranted.

"Come sit down here at the table and slowly tell me again what happened. Stop crying."

He questioned me about Mr. Tyler. What kind of grades did I get in his class? Did I do my homework like I was supposed to? Did I turn in assignments on time? Dad said that I should not have been talking in class, and I should not have talked back to Mr. Tyler after he told me to sit down.

"After he tore up your test paper, you didn't need to say anything else. After class you should have gone to the counselor's office and told them that I'd be up there. You know I won't uphold you when you do wrong. School is no place to play. I send you there to get an education, and you know how to behave yourself. But I think that teacher was wrong. I'll be up there. I'm going to look into this."

The next afternoon I was called to the counselor's office. Dad, Mr. Tyler, and the counselor were there. Dad must have left work early because he still had his uniform on. Everyone looked serious when I entered the room. Mr. Tyler spoke first. He said that all the students knew that there was not to be any talking while the tests were being graded. I interrupted to explain why I was talking. Dad turned to me and said in a calm, stern voice, "Listen and let him finish."

Mr. Tyler continued and said something to the effect that I really surprised him because I was usually so polite and a very good student. He hoped that we could put all this behind us and end the year on a positive note. I kept quiet. Dad asked, "Since her test paper was torn up, how is that going to affect her grade in your class? Are you going to count it against her?"

"Oh, no, Mr. Streeter, it will be as if she was absent. The test won't count against her in any way," Mr. Tyler said.

I was excused but everyone else remained seated. Before I left the room, Dad said, "I'll see you when you get home." I got the hint that I wasn't to wait for him to leave the meeting.

Our family did not have a car. Dad came up to school that afternoon, without an appointment, on the bus and subway. Later, when I went to Mr. Tyler's class, he never looked in my direction. For the remainder of the year, I went to class and did my work. Mr. Tyler often ignored my hand when I raised it to answer a question. He only called on me when no one else raised their hand. At the end of the semester, I got a good grade.

* * *

When the time to graduate from junior high school approached, I had a decision to make. Would I go to Simon Gratz High School, the predominantly black school in my neighborhood, or request a transfer to a predominantly white high school outside the neighborhood? There was no doubt that Mom and Dad were serious about all of us getting a good education, no matter how far we had to travel, the institutional obstacles, or the prejudice. It was 1966; the Civil Rights Act was passed last summer, civil rights marches were occurring throughout the South for better jobs, the right to vote, and quality education. People were dying for justice and equal opportunity. But my dream was Dad's fight, and he was in it for the long haul. I applied for a transfer from Gratz High to attend to Roxborough High. Dad was adamant that I was not going to Gratz because he had heard that the graduation rate was low and it was not highly regarded academically. My transfer papers were submitted to the Board of Education.

Before the transfer was approved, Dr. Marcus A. Foster, a black man, the new principal at Gratz, called my parents. Dr. Foster was a man of vision. He had accepted the challenge to turn around this neighborhood high school where the dropout rate was two times greater than the rate of graduation. He set out to prove that hard work and high expectations make a difference. He knew that children from impoverished families dreamed dreams far beyond the expectations that others had for them.

Dr. Foster was aware that my parents had requested a transfer, and he asked to meet with them before a final decision was made. Dad agreed to meet with him. During the meeting Dr. Foster told Dad about his plans to make changes to improve Gratz. He intended to institute a motivation program and other advanced courses for the top 10% of the entering 10th grade class. These courses would include before- and after-school classes. There would be Saturday classes to prepare for the SAT, and cultural and professional enrichment activities such as plays, trips, and meetings with professionals in the community. Around the dinner table that evening, Dad told us about his meeting with Dr. Foster. Dad told Dr. Foster that I wanted to be a lawyer. He told him that I needed a good education so that I could go to college and then on to law school. Dr. Foster understood my father's concern. I later learned that he had a daughter my age. He assured Dad that he would see to it that I received a scholarship when I graduated. Dr. Foster told him, "If your daughter keeps up the good work and gets good grades, she'll do just fine. I give you my word."

When the meeting ended, Dad told Dr. Foster, "If I let my daughter come to Gratz and you don't deliver on your promises or if there is any other foolishness at that school, I'm going to pull her out of there. And if I pull her out, the Board of Education better transfer her to a good school."

After Dad finished telling us about the meeting, he turned to me.

"You gonna go to Gratz in September. I think that man is sincere and you'll be alright. But I meant what I told him. If there is any foolishness at that school, I will pull you out."

I was surprised that Dad changed his mind. But if he said it was okay, it was fine with me. I looked forward to going to high school with my old friends. After junior high school, I really wasn't looking forward to going to Roxborough High. Also, Dr. Foster knew that my father expected him to deliver on everything he promised.

In 1969, more than 800 students graduated from Simon Gratz High School, the largest class ever to graduate, and one-third of our class went on to college. I was the class valedictorian.

Almost 40 years after I graduated from Gratz I was asked to speak at a dedication ceremony at Cheyney State University in honor of Dr. Foster. A teacher who coached basketball at Gratz when I was there came up to me and said that he remembered me because I was in the first class after Dr. Foster was appointed principal. He said that Dr. Foster told him that he was as determined to recruit outstanding academic talent to attend Gratz as the coaches were to recruit the best athletes.

2

Respect

Long before I went to high school, Dad taught all of his children lessons that we would need not just to make it through school, but to survive.

Dad set standards for how he and everyone in our family was to be treated and how we were to conduct ourselves. He taught us, "Do unto others as you want others to do unto you. What that means is, treat people the way you want to be treated." He always made sure that we understood what he told us. He would say, "Let me break it down for you." Dad told us, "If you treat people with respect, you have a right to be treated with respect." There was an unspoken but often demonstrated subtext with this advice. When you treat someone with respect and they disrespect you, then you had a right to stand up and call to their attention how you expected to be treated. Dad told all of us, "Nobody has a right to disrespect you or walk over you."

As I got older and my circle of friends expanded beyond the kids on the block and those with whom I went to school, I discovered that everyone was not taught how to show respect for themselves or anyone else. When these friends came in contact with Dad, their lack of knowledge caused serious problems for them and for me.

It was late winter of 1965. I was 13 years old. Mom and I were on our way to the grocery store. On Friday evenings after dinner, Mom and I usually walked to the A&P market which was three blocks from where we lived. I enjoyed our walks to the market because I had Mom all to myself and talked to her about anything I wanted to know without anyone interrupting us. That evening I had something very important to ask her.

"Mom, when can I 'take boy company'?"

This was a phrase I had heard her use for when a boy could come to the house to see me. We both understood that this was a first step toward my having a boyfriend. She slowed her stride and quickly glanced in my direction. I could tell by the expression on her face she was thinking, *Now what's this all about?*

"I guess when you're about fifteen or sixteen." She resumed her pace.

I swallowed hard. She turned to face me and watched my reaction. We stopped walking. This topic was groundbreaking; getting to the market could wait.

"When do you think you should be allowed to take boy company?"

"Well, I kind of thought tomorrow."

Now, I wasn't sure this was a good time to bring this subject up, but I had already kind of told the boy he could come over tomorrow. Mom's brow furrowed; she grimaced and started walking faster than usual.

"I'm not so sure about that. I think you're too young to be seeing anybody."

From the tone of her voice, I knew she wasn't enjoying this conversation, but she knew she had to make a decision and give me an answer.

"But I'd rather you bring the boy to the house than to meet him somewhere in the street. So you can have him come over tomorrow."

We didn't talk about much of anything else on the way to or back from the market.

Charles was the boy. Everyone called him Buck; Black

Buck, to be exact. He was about 6'1", much taller than my dad. Buck usually wore a greasy black "do-rag" on his processed hair. That night when he came to see me, his do-rag was stuffed in the back pocket of his jeans. I saw the greasy ends hanging out from his pocket. Buck came with his "roady" (good friend) Cockroach, who we called Roach for short. Everyone in my family was at home: my two younger sisters, Ellen, age seven, and Marilyn, who we called Reese, age four, and Jeanette, my older sister, age 21. Jeanette was mentally retarded, the term used at that time for anyone with significant cognitive deficits. She stayed close by when anyone came to visit and usually played with my younger sisters. Mom was in the kitchen, and Dad was upstairs in his bedroom. My brother, Johnny, age 14, was on his way out to meet up with his friends.

Johnny didn't want Buck or any of the guys in the neighborhood coming to see me. Buck wasn't concerned about Johnny. He was 16 and considered Johnny just one of the "young boys" in the hood. Buck was a tough guy; he had been arrested and had a reputation in the neighborhood as someone not to be messed with. I certainly had not told Mom about any of that. On his way out the door, Johnny greeted Buck with an icy coolness reserved for an unwanted guest. "Hey, man, how you doin'." He slapped hands with Roach and went out the door. Roach went into the dining room to keep my sisters amused so that Buck and I could be alone in the living room. We lived in a two-story row house; the first floor was a "straight through." From the door to the vestibule, one entered the living room, which opened into the dining room, which led to the kitchen.

I knew Mom had told Dad that "some boy" was coming over to see me. But Dad never mentioned anything about it to me. After about an hour, Dad came downstairs. When he reached the bottom of the steps, I immediately stood up to introduce Charles to him. No way was I going to introduce him to Dad as Buck. Buck slowly, without any enthusiasm, partially lifted his lanky frame from the sofa and kind of extended his hand and mumbled as he looked down at the floor in front of Dad. "Hey, how you doin'?"

I am sure Buck was not accustomed to meeting fathers of girls he was interested in. This was new to him. He probably thought that he was doing the right thing. After all, he almost stood up and made an attempt to extend his hand.

Dad didn't think very much of boys or men who processed their hair. He called them "hoodlums" or "slicksters." At that moment I was glad that Dad couldn't see the ends of the do-rag hanging from Buck's pocket. He was two feet away from the sofa when Buck mumbled his greeting. The look on Dad's face was as if Buck had spit on him. He quickly looked Buck up and down from head to toe, twice. Then Dad walked his sturdy, well-built, 5'10" frame, shoulders erect, head tilted up, so that his nose was directly in Buck's face and slowly repeated Buck's greeting.

"'Hey, how you doin'?"

The cold, dark look in Dad's eyes left no doubt that he found Buck and everything about him totally unacceptable. In a harsh tone, dripping with contempt, Dad said, "You don't address me like that. You're not my equal. When you're in my house, you say good evening, good afternoon, or whatever the case may be, Mr. Streeter [with emphasis on his name]. Do you understand?"

Now Buck stood up straight.

"Yes, sir."

It was as if he was addressing a commanding officer in the military. Dad walked away and went to the kitchen without a word and without acknowledging Buck's still-outstretched hand. Buck slowly sat down on the edge of the sofa and shook his head. Still in shock, he let out a deep breath and said, "Your Pop's a tough man."

I was speechless. We sat staring in the direction of the TV for few minutes before Buck abruptly called to Roach, "Come on, man, let's go. Kathy, I'll catch you later."

And with that, my first boy company visit ended.

After Buck and Roach left, I went to the kitchen, where Mom and Dad sat at the kitchen table. In an incredulous whisper I asked Dad, "Why did you do that?"

Dad gave me a penetrating look, serious but not angry. In hindsight, I guess he wondered why I didn't understand.

"Do you understand that that boy talked to me like I was one of the boys on the corner? I am your father and an adult. He will give me respect. If he doesn't show me respect, it will only be a matter of time before he disrespects you. I meant what I said. And if he doesn't like it, he don't have to come here, and you won't be seeing him anywhere else either."

End of discussion. Buck never again came to my house and was never mentioned by Dad after that night.

Later, when Johnny came home, he looked around and asked, "Where's Buck and Roach?"

I told him what happened when I introduced Buck to Dad. Johnny laughed hard and fell on the floor. He kept laughing and asked me over and over again to show him how "Dad stepped into Buck's grill." Then he said, "Well, sis, I guess you gonna have to find a new boyfriend."

News of Dad's encounter with Buck got around the neighborhood. As a result, I had a decision to make: pursue my desire to be popular, especially in the eyes of one of the toughest guys in the neighborhood, or, without apologizing or complaining, stand by my father's actions. I knew that I had to obey my father. No matter how tough Buck's reputation was in the neighborhood, he knew my father was not afraid. I don't know if Dad was aware of Buck's reputation, but it wouldn't have made a difference in the respect he demanded.

After that incident, I thought everybody was talking about what happened between my dad and Buck. But that was not the case at all. Some people knew and didn't care. For others, it was just a passing piece of humorous gossip. I didn't have to worry about "boy company" for a long time. The next time a boy from the neighborhood asked to come to see me, he was very well informed, by rumors which had been blown way out of proportion, about how to address my dad and the respect he demanded.

* * *

Even though I saw how Dad responded when visitors to our home failed to show respect, there came a time when I had to get a personal lesson.

January 1968, on an extremely cold, overcast winter evening, the mustard-colored leather trench coat that Mom and Dad bought me for Christmas looked good, but it didn't keep me warm enough when the bus didn't come as scheduled. I had to walk 16 blocks from Broad Street to 30th Street, where we lived. I was 15, with a sharp tongue and full of adolescent attitude. That evening after school, I was cold and disgusted at the world. When I came in the house, Dad was sitting in his usual chair next to the lamp in the living room, reading the newspaper and waiting for Mom to finish cooking dinner. The delicious aroma of spaghetti sauce chocked with onions, garlic, Italian seasonings, and stewed tomatoes which had been simmering all day filled the air. Spaghetti and meatballs were a family favorite. Neither the warmth inside the house nor the anticipated great dinner quelled my anger. That week Dad was working the midnight to 8 a.m. shift. Our family would eat dinner together, and Dad would go back to bed for a few hours before he had to get up and go to work.

I almost, but not quite, slammed the front door and stomped past Dad without a word. I went to the dining room and dropped my books on the table. My fingers felt like popsicles and were stinging from the bitter cold. I quickly unfastened the buttons on that cold leather coat, which I couldn't escape fast enough.

Dad looked up slowly from his newspaper and stared at

me over the thick black rim of his reading glasses. I felt him looking at me even before I cast my eyes in his direction. Haltingly Dad said, "Young lady, have you seen me before today?"

I looked at him and, with all the anger I had for the bus driver who caused me to walk those 16 blocks and with venom, I spewed, "Look, I am cold; I had to walk all the way home."

In an instant Dad leaped from his chair, the newspaper splayed across the living room floor, and he pounced into the dining room. With one hand he grabbed me by the collar of that coat, which he and Mom sacrificed to buy for me, and hurled me across the living room. I landed in a heap on the sofa. My eyes stretched wide and my once bold and angry voice was silent. In a booming voice he said, "Do you know who you're talking to? I'm your father."

I didn't move as I struggled to understand how he threw me across the room and my feet never touched the floor. Before I could say anything—not that I *wanted* to say anything—Mom came running from the kitchen. "What's going on? Alright, alright, wait a minute, Streeter." That is what Mom called Dad.

Dad roared, "She is not going to talk to me like that. I'll break her neck. Who does she think I am?"

Sternly Mom said, "Kathy, go upstairs to your room, right now."

Relieved to escape from Dad, I bolted upstairs to my room.

Mom continued to try and calm Dad. "I don't know what's got into her. Look, dinner is almost ready." Dad ranted on but Mom had taken control of the situation.

Another coal added to fuel my anger; I seethed as I lay across my bed.

About an hour later, Mom came upstairs to my room. "What's wrong with you today? You know better than to talk to your father like that."

I began to explain about the bus and the cold. But before I

said more than a few words, Mom shook her head and said, in that firm tone she used when she wasn't interested in hearing any more, "I don't care about none of that. You don't ever disrespect your father. He does too much for you, for you to talk to him like that. Now I want you to beg his pardon. Do you understand me?"

Now my feelings were hurt. Mom had come down on me too. But worse, I had disrespected Dad. Tears burned my eyes and flowed over my face. Now I was angry at myself.

Dad had come upstairs and was in bed reading the *Reader's Digest* before he went to sleep. I stood in the doorway to his bedroom and watched him for a few minutes. I thought, *Suppose he's still mad at me and doesn't want to see me or hear anything I have to say?* My chest heaved as I took in shallow breaths and the tears came faster. In a voice barely loud enough to be heard as the words stuck on the lump in my throat, I said, "Daddy, I'm sorry." This tone was very different from the hormonal 15-year-old on fire with anger just a few hours ago.

He looked over at me still standing in the doorway and said, "Come here."

I ran over and laid my head on his shoulder and cried as if I'd lost the most precious thing I ever had. "Daddy, I'm sorry. I didn't mean to disrespect you."

"I accept your apology. Go ahead and cry, your daddy's got big shoulders."

I cried and he patted my head. After a couple of minutes, he pushed me away, kissed me on the forehead, and said, "Now get out of here. I got to get some sleep."

I always remembered that while Dad forgave my inappropriate behavior, he did not say that what I did was alright. His actions left no doubt that he was displeased, and Mom's heart-to-heart discipline reinforced Dad's position. I learned that disrespect would not be tolerated by Mom or Dad, and I couldn't play one against the other. Respect was not negotiable.

3

Think For Yourself

September 1966, my first day in high school, I sat with Pauline and Anne, two of my best friends. Pauline lived on my block, and Anne lived around the corner on Oakdale Street. We were friends since elementary school and saw each other every day. We were excited as we rode the bus to Simon Gratz High School. The new freshman class assembled in the auditorium, and I sat between Anne and Pauline. Because I was sent to school out of our neighborhood to attend junior high school, this was the first time we would be in school together again. There were more than 1,000 10th graders in the class of 78/69; the number 78 was the number of the class at Simon Gratz and 69 represented the year we expected to graduate. The auditorium was packed beyond capacity. Everyone was waving, screaming, and hugging friends they had not seen over the summer. Noise and laughter filled the cavernous auditorium; we were glad to be in high school and all together again. Public schools in Philadelphia in 1966 did not have air-conditioning. Even with the windows open and huge, loud fans set at the highest speeds, it was scorching hot in that auditorium. But it didn't matter; we had made it to high school.

Dr. Foster, the principal, came on stage, stood behind the podium, and looked around the room. He stood up straight.

He had on a dark, three-piece suit, a tie, and a starched white shirt. He wore thick, round, wire-rimmed glasses. That's how he looked the first day of school and every day thereafter. After a few minutes he calmly but forcefully spoke into the microphone; he repeatedly asked my rowdy classmates to settle down and take their seats. With assistance from teachers and staff interspersed throughout the room, the noise subsided and everyone sat down.

Dr. Foster said, "Look to your right and now look to your left. Only one of you is expected to graduate from high school. That's what people are saying. Together, we are going to prove them wrong." His tone was serious and defiant.

Now the room was quiet; even the whispering stopped. Shock and apprehension replaced joy and excitement. As we sat with our friends, an unasked question crossed our minds: Who was not going to make it to graduation? I knew that I had to take a lot of classes to get from the first day of 10th grade to graduation. But I had no idea that much of what I needed to learn in order to make it through would be lessons taught outside the classroom.

* * *

"This is my house; me and your mother make the rules. As long as you live under my roof, you'll follow the rules. If you don't like it, when you get grown, you get your own house and live by your own rules. You understand me?" Growing up, that's what Dad told me, my brother, and my sisters many times. The rules applied to all of us and there were no exceptions. Dad did not spare the rod when we disobeyed the rules.

Even though I knew the rules, I still tried to walk close to the line. When I was in high school, I didn't want to be labeled "square" or a "young girl" by my friends or any of the older kids. I was skipped a grade in elementary school and was younger than the kids in my class. Near the end of my first semester, before first period class, I hung outside the building, in front of "Jack's," the corner delicatessen across the street from the school. I stayed out there with older students until the very last minute before the late bell rang. Then I ran as fast as I could to get to class before I was marked late. The kids I wanted to impress didn't care about being late for school. But I knew that when I got my report card, first Dad would look at the record of absences and lateness before he looked at my grades. I went to school early enough not to be late.

Students who cut class to hang out in the cafeteria or to go home early were considered "cool." I wanted to appear to be doing the same things as the "cool kids." Often I went to class and asked the teacher to be excused for a few minutes to go to the bathroom or the counselor's office. Because I was a good student, my homework was always done and I participated in class, the teacher usually let me go. Before I returned to class, I went to the cafeteria. Anyone who knew that I wasn't supposed to be there would think that I was cutting class—just like the cool kids. I knew that I'd better not get caught, Dad better not find out, and my grades better not suffer. It was hard playing close to the line.

It was near the end of the second semester, the last period of the day, and I was leaving the building with a few of my friends. We wanted to get home in time to watch *Dark Shadows*, our favorite show on television. Earlier that day I told one of the gym teachers that I had to go to the counselor's office and would not be in gym class. I expected to be excused and didn't bother to go to see if my request was granted. Many of my friends who cut class didn't bother concocting excuses or getting passes like I did. We were laughing and talking and were almost out of the building when my name was broadcast over the public address system. Everyone stopped; all eyes were on me when Mrs. Richardson, my gym teacher, said sternly over the loudspeaker, "If Kathryn Streeter is in the building, she is to report to the gym immediately. No more notes or excuses for her to get out of gym class will be honored for the remainder of the year."

Damn! I took off like an Olympic sprinter in the last leg of the 440 relay. I ran to my locker, which was on the fourth floor, and grabbed my sneakers and my much-wrinkled blue gym suit, which had not been worn or washed in months. I ran immediately to the gym, which was located in the basement, and went to Mrs. Richardson's office. Out of breath and panting, I said, "Mrs. Richardson, why did you embarrass me like that?" My tone was not disrespectful but I was surprised. Mrs. Richardson knew that I was a good student.

She leaned back in her chair, looked at me over her half-rimmed eyeglasses with a cold, no-nonsense stare and, in an implacable tone, said, "I see from the attendance records you have an excuse for one thing or another for every gym class that is scheduled at the end of the day. No more, young lady. Now do I need to call your parents about this? I know you're on the honor roll, but you won't be if you flunk physical education."

Speechless, I searched for something to say to get back on her good side. My thoughts raced but I couldn't think of anything. Mrs. Richardson's eyes locked on mine as she waited for me to say something. She had caught on to my game, and now she played the winning cards—call my parents, flunk physical education, and not make the honor roll. That was it. From that moment it was clear that I wouldn't be home in time to see *Dark Shadows* anymore.

My choices were to follow the crowd and try to be one of the "cool kids" or go to gym, stay on the honor roll, and not get on Dad's bad side. I knew that I was no exception to the rules that Dad told us. He couldn't care less if I was one of the cool kids. I didn't want to find out what punishment I was in for if Dad ever found out that I cut class or that I didn't make the honor roll because of it. The things I did to be considered one of the cool kids required me to ignore something that Dad constantly told me and my brother, Johnny: "Think for yourself, don't just follow the crowd." I paid attention when Johnny learned the hard way that this was not a suggestion but a requirement.

* * *

In the early 1960s it was the style for teenage boys and young men to process their hair. This required them to use chemicals to make their hair slick and shiny. One evening after dinner I sat on the front steps with Johnny, age 13, and a few of his friends. A group of older guys with processed hair passed by our house. Dad was sitting in one of the three red rocking chairs on the porch, talking to Mr. Smith, our next-door neighbor. Johnny was impressed by everything about these guys: the way they strolled, the slang they used, and most of all, their processed hairstyles.

"You see their 'dos'? Now that's boss. I'm gonna get me a process. I want a Quo Vadis," Johnny boasted.

That was the name of one of the popular processed hairstyles. Before Johnny finished bragging about how good he would look with a Quo Vadis, Dad said, in a tone that left no doubt that he did not approve, "Boy, don't you let anybody put that 'conk' in your hair. You don't have to follow the crowd. You better think for yourself. But I don't care what nobody else does, you better not put that mess in your hair."

I thought that was the end of that. Dad had spoken.

About a month later, on a Saturday afternoon, Johnny came in the house and his hair was processed. He told me that Morty, an older boy who lived across the street, processed his hair and his friend Harold's hair. Johnny told me that the stuff Morty used to straighten their hair burned like hell, but that Morty told them to run around the block as fast as they could a couple of times before he took it out. Johnny grinned as he strutted back and forth in front of the large wall mirror in the dining room.

"You just wait until Dad sees it," I said.

Johnny avoided Dad and Mom all day. I lurked around the house because I didn't want to miss the first moment when Dad saw Johnny's hair. Late that afternoon Dad was in the living room, and Johnny came in the house from the backyard and quietly went through the kitchen and skulked down the steps to the basement. We never came in the house from the backyard. It was time for dinner; Dad came into the kitchen and asked Mom, "Where is Johnny? I haven't seen him much today."

Dinner on Saturdays was a lot less structured than during the week and on Sundays. On Saturdays we usually ate sandwiches or hot dogs and baked beans, and the family didn't always eat together.

"He must be outside. I haven't seen him since this morning," Mom said.

Dad squinted; he suspected something. He turned and asked me, "Have you seen Johnny?"

"I think he's down in the basement."

"Johnny, Johnny, come up here, boy," Dad hollered down the basement steps.

Slowly Johnny came upstairs, not running as he usually did. When he got to the doorway, it only took a minute before Dad's eyes zeroed in on his head. Johnny didn't look as confident as he had earlier. He was scared but he stood up straight, held his head up, and looked Dad in the eye.

When Mom saw Johnny's hair, she gasped, "Oh, for goodness sakes, what did you do to your hair?"

Dad pushed back from the kitchen table with force. The screech of the kitchen chair on the linoleum floor was loud, rough, and fast. Dad leaped up, grabbed Johnny by his shirt collar, and pulled it tight around his neck. Through clenched teeth he said, "I told you not to put that mess in your hair, didn't I? You gonna listen to me or those hoodlums in the street? I'll break your neck."

Dad yanked Johnny down to the basement. He found the dark-brown lye soap that Mom used to get tough stains out of clothes, and he scrubbed Johnny's scalp until the chemicals were washed out. Next, he took a pair of scissors and cut off any straight hair that remained. All evidence of the Quo Vadis that Johnny sported so proudly earlier in the afternoon was gone. Johnny's head was a "hot mess." The lye soap burned his scalp and later caused sores. Dad, like the guys who put that mess in Johnny's hair, didn't know anything about chemical reactions or hair treatments. After Johnny was "de-Quo Vadised," Dad called him from the basement and told him to sit down in the living room. I listened from the kitchen.

"Look, boy, you better learn how to think for yourself. Those guys out there with that slick hair, looking like hoodlums, don't have anything going for themselves. Is that what you want, to be a hoodlum and probably end up in jail?" Dad said.

Johnny sat still, his eyes dark red from crying, shoulders slumped down, and he sniffed as he mumbled softly, "No, I just want my hair to be in style."

"Damn the style!" Dad shouted. "You set the style for yourself. You don't follow behind a bunch of dummies like them hoodlums. Best you learn that now. You better think for yourself and don't just follow the crowd. But never mind that—I told you not to put that mess in your hair, didn't I?"

"Yes."

"You gonna learn to listen to me, your daddy, not those hoodlums in the street. You're on punishment for the next month. Now, if your hoodlum friends got something to say about your hair, you tell them to come see me."

Johnny never applied chemicals to his hair again. After he became an adult, Johnny was a style trendsetter in the neighborhood. Unfortunately, the lesson Dad tried to teach from this experience did not take the first time. Like many guys in the neighborhood, Johnny became addicted to drugs after he graduated from high school.

* * *

As teenagers Johnny and I often had to choose which path to follow. Mom and Dad had the first opportunity to teach us how to make choices. Dad told us, "Think for yourself. Don't follow the crowd. Do what you know to be right." They taught us the difference between right and wrong. But the crowd and the forces in the street were unrelenting in charting a different course for us to follow. Dad didn't back down, even when he had to battle us for our own good.

4

Fighting Foolishness

Before Dad relented and let me go to Gratz, the neighborhood high school, he told Dr. Foster if there was any foolishness at that school, he was going to pull me out of there. There wasn't a specific definition for what Dad considered foolishness. But I understood that foolishness was anything that distracted me or prevented me from getting a good education. Dad often said he didn't put up with foolishness, which was a catch-all phrase that included anything he didn't approve of. There was plenty of foolishness at Gratz and in my neighborhood, but I never wanted to leave either place.

I was in the 11th grade. It was a couple of months into the school year. Dad's car pulled up quickly to the curb in front of the school. He yelled, "Kathy, get in the car!"

I froze and my eyes opened wide. What was he doing here? He never picked me up from school.

Pauline, Anne, and I had just come out of the building and planned to meet our friends to go home together on the bus. Rumors had spread throughout school all day that girls from our neighborhood, who we called the Wolfpack, were coming to school to fight us. A few of the Wolfpack went to Gratz, but most of them sporadically attended other schools in the city. I, along with seven of my friends, belonged to a social club called "Club Revlon," and most of us went to Gratz. Since only a few of the Wolfpack attended Gratz, I relaxed at school and didn't worry about dirty looks, being called names or bumped into in the halls. But that day, the neighborhood feud came to school, and all hell was expected to break loose. The tension throughout the day felt like the percussion of drums that got louder, faster, and harder as the time to leave school approached.

* * *

The girls in Club Revlon often dressed alike at parties and attracted attention with choreographed dance routines that we created and performed. We liked the attention, especially from the boys. That's when some of the girls who lived in the area became our enemies. The boys in the neighborhood began calling them the Wolfpack. The summer before I started 11th grade, there were a few fights between members of Club Revlon and the Wolfpack. I got into a fight with Sandy, one of the Wolfpack, after she scrawled *Fuck Kathy, Sandy and Harvey 4ever* on the wall of Big Ernie's pool room, which was located on the corner of the block where I lived. Harvey was my boyfriend but he used to go with Sandy before he went into the Army.

Some girls in the Wolfpack were known to carry knives and box cutters. My friend Shirley, also a member of Club Revlon, and I decided to carry metal chains in paper bags for protection. We didn't want to carry anything that our parents considered a weapon, but we didn't want to be empty-handed if the Wolfpack caught one of us alone.

A couple of days before the Wolfpack came to Gratz, an NTA (non-teaching assistant) came and got me out of class. "They want you in Mr. Ruffin's office, and bring those chains with you," he said.

Mr. Ruffin was the vice principal. I walked to my locker and got the wrinkled brown paper bag that I carried my chains in. I was surprised that the NTA had come for me, but

I was more surprised that Mr. Ruffin, or anyone aside from my close friends, knew about the chains. I hoped that they didn't find out about the chains because the Wolfpack had caught Shirley alone and she had to use her chains on them. I trembled inside, afraid that I was in big trouble. I planned to explain to Mr. Ruffin that I had to protect myself. The boys in the neighborhood warned me to watch my back.

I walked cautiously into Mr. Ruffin's office. I halted as I entered the office. I was surprised to see Dad there. He knew about the fights that took place over the summer and that a few of the girls who wanted to fight me went to Gratz. Dad was the one who told Mr. Ruffin that I was carrying chains in a bag to protect myself. Like a flash of light, I knew instantly how Dad knew so much about what was going on. Mom told Dad everything. I never told Mom anything about the fights, but she was home one Saturday afternoon last summer when Sammy, who lived around the corner, broke up the fight between Sandy and me. The day of the fight, Sammy put me in a head lock and wrestled with me as he dragged me home.

"Kathy, I'm takin' you home. You ain't fighin' them. They're just waitin' to jump you. Now stop fighting me and come on." He argued with me as he pushed and pulled me down the street to get me home.

Just as he pushed me into my house, five girls, members of the Wolfpack, came running from around the corner and stood across the street from my house. They yelled, "Let her go, let her go! Come back outside. We gonna kick your ass."

Mom heard the shouting and ran to the door. She wanted to know who those girls were and what was this all about. I gave her the response that a 15-year-old gave parents who asked questions about "my business": "It's nothing, just some stupid girls trying to start something!"

All summer the feud continued to escalate, and Mom hovered in the background, taking in everything that my friends and I talked about daily.

Mr. Ruffin asked me about the fights that happened over

the summer and if anyone threatened me in school. I told him that a few weeks ago, Sheila, who was in the Wolfpack, and two other girls who I didn't know surrounded me in the stairwell when I was on my way to class. He wanted to know the names of all the girls in Club Revlon and the Wolfpack, and where everyone lived. Vice Principal Ruffin assured Dad that he would look into this and that I would be safe in school. He also told Dad that I had to stop carrying chains. Mr. Ruffin told me to let him know if anything happened outside or in school between any of the girls in Club Revlon and the Wolfpack or any other girls.

Dad nodded his head, bit his bottom lip, and in a tone that let Mr. Ruffin and everyone in the room know that he was not satisfied, he said, "Alright, she is not going to carry chains or anything else. I'll make sure of that. But nobody better do anything here to hurt her. I want you to make sure she's safe in this school. I don't send her here to get into fights. Something has got to be done about this before somebody gets hurt."

* * *

Now it was two days after that meeting with Mr. Ruffin. Dad yelled again, "Kathy, you heard me, get in the car now!"

I heard yelling behind me. I turned around and saw Gaye, one of my friends, come out of the building. About ten girls were across the street screaming, "Oh yeah, yeah! We're here for your asses. C'mon out."

It was the Wolfpack. One of their leaders, Big Paula, ran into the middle of the street. Traffic screeched to a halt, and cars swerved to avoid hitting her. Gaye, cursing, ran into the street to meet her.

"Mr. Streeter, you want us to get in the car too?" Anne asked Dad as she kept looking back at the brawl that ignited when Gaye ran into the street.

"Yeah, you and Pauline, all of you get in here," Dad said.

Anne didn't have to be told a second time. She hopped quickly into the back seat, and with a sound of scared relief in her voice, she yelled to me, "Kathy, now listen to your father. Come on, get in." Anne didn't want anything to do with this fight.

I looked back toward the crowd that had surrounded Gaye and Big Paula. I took a step in the direction of the fight. Dad shouted in a menacing, no-nonsense tone that said without words, *Don't make me come get you*, "You heard me. Get in here, now!"

I got in the car, closed the door, and then I heard sirens. Two unmarked cars with flashing lights drove into the crowd. Dad drove away and took us home. I found out later that the men in the unmarked cars were from the Police Department's Juvenile Aid Division and the girls involved in the fight were taken to the police station.

Dad was quiet during dinner. What happened at school was not discussed around the dinner table. Before dinner my brother, Johnny, and I talked about it. All the kids in the neighborhood knew about the fight and who was arrested.

After dinner Dad told me to come upstairs, he wanted to talk to me. He asked me why didn't I tell him when all this mess first started. I shrugged my shoulders. "I don't know."

But I knew why. I wanted to handle it myself, and I didn't want to run to my mommy and daddy when girls who didn't like me threatened to beat me up. But I didn't say any of that to Dad.

He wanted an explanation but when I didn't say anything else, he asked, "Why didn't you get in the car when I told you the first time?"

I stared at the floor for a few minutes before I looked into his eyes. "Dad, I can't run from them. If they think I'm scared, I'll always be running."

All during dinner and when he began asking me questions, Dad looked disgusted. Now he looked sad. "They know you not scared because you fought one of them already. They know you'll fight. But you got to understand that all they want to do is to bring you down to their level or try and hurt you. You gotta be smarter than them. Use your head [he pointed to his head], not your fists [held up his fists]. People who can't think use their fists first. You're smarter than that. I told you to use your head and think first. Do you understand what I'm sayin' to you?"

"Yes."

"Look, you can't get upset because people talk about you or don't like you. I bet most of those girls don't even know you. You can't control what people say or think. You know who you are, and what they say about you don't change anything. Some people say stuff just to get under your skin and make you mad. Ignore them. Don't let them control you. They may want to fight you. But ain't nothin' they can do if you ignore them. If they put their hands on you, then you have the right to fight back. But before it comes to that, tell somebody who can take care of it. I'm your daddy, you can come to me. Alright? If there is any more trouble, I want to know about it. You understand me?"

"Yes."

Things at school got back to normal, and there were no more fights in the neighborhood.

As a result of this incident, Dad learned a lesson that he may not have been ready for: I would no longer run to him to fight my battles. This didn't make him happy, but it was a consequence of my growing up. As best he could before I left home, he wanted to teach me how to deal with people and situations determined to bring me down. He didn't want me to be afraid or too prideful to ask for help when I needed it. Most important, he wanted me to know that he was always there for me.

5

Don't Ride the Red Horse

Dad studied all of his children closely. He searched for our strengths and weaknesses. And he asked all of us, "What do you want to be when you grow up?" I thought it was just small talk that grown-ups had with children. As I look back, I appreciate that this question had a purpose. Dad assumed that we would grow up physically and emotionally and not be killed off or our spirits broken during our youth. Such a simple question, asked over and over again, made us think about the future, set goals, and make plans. Dad didn't engage in idle feel-good conversations. Whatever we wanted to do in life, he planned to help and be there for us.

* * *

Growing up, I had a quick temper and a sharp tongue. When I got angry with my classmates, teachers, my brother, sisters, or friends, Dad sat me down and asked what happened to make me so angry.

"Who are you mad at? What did they do? And what did you do before they did that?"

He listened. If he thought I was wrong, he told me. If he thought I had a reason to be angry, he suggested how I should handle the situation. The most difficult thing he made me do was honestly ask myself what responsibility I had for the situation that made me so angry. Dad was keenly perceptive and helped me to analyze situations thoroughly. It wasn't until I stopped to think, which often meant looking at situations from more than just my perspective, that I could think clearly and consider what to do next. When confronted with tense situations and with a full head of steam, I often prepared to charge forward in the wrong direction.

In high school I ran for senior class president and lost the election by a small number of votes. It was rumored that the election was unfair because some of the seniors were away on a school trip, and most of them would have voted for me. And I was told that some friends of my opponent counted the votes. A few of my friends and I told our teachers about what we heard, angrily expressed our views that the election was unfair, and demanded a new election. The teachers listened and attempted to calm us down but refused to hold a new election. I was furious and didn't understand the teachers' response to our demand for a new election. I decided if that's the way it was going to be, then I wouldn't participate in anything else at school. I'd just go to class, do my work, and nothing else.

That evening at dinner, I told Dad about the election, how I was cheated, and what I planned to do. As always, Dad let me tell my side in full rage, and then he said, "Perhaps all the students who were on that trip wouldn't have voted for you. Maybe you still might not have won the election. Did you think about that?"

I didn't answer because I'd never thought about that.

"If there was a new election and you won this time, the students who supported the other student would probably say that election wasn't fair. I am not making excuses for the teachers or what happened, but let's think about what you're plannin' to do. Who you gonna hurt by quitting everything? The kids who you think cheated won't care if you quit everything that you're involved in at school. Will they?"

I kept quiet and listened. I really didn't want to hear anything except support for my indignation. I wanted Dad to give me the green light to do something to get back at everybody, especially those who I believed stole the election and the teachers who refused to do anything about it. Dad understood my silence. He knew I wasn't ready to concede that my decision to quit everything wasn't a good idea.

"Look, you think about what you plannin' to do. But remember, 'Don't ride the red horse.'"

My brow furrowed. I had heard Dad use that expression before, but I'd never asked what it meant.

"Do you know what that means?"

I shook my head. "No."

"It means that you are about to make a decision or do something when you're mad. You're acting out of anger, without thinking. You should never do that. I've always told you 'think before you act.' In this situation you don't want to ride the red horse."

I left Dad sitting at the kitchen table and went upstairs to my room. I lay across the bed, still angry but now thinking. The students who supported me wouldn't want me to quit because of the cheaters. And the cheaters would think that they hurt my feelings and backed me down. Even worse, they would think that they "took my heart." And because of them, I'd be afraid to speak up for the things that I thought should be done senior year. I thought, *Oh yeah, they got another thing coming*. Dad was right, I did think better when I wasn't angry.

Dad was always on the alert. He stepped in whenever it looked as if my temper was about to consume me. On several occasions he said, "Hold on a minute, be careful. Looks to me like you're riding the red horse.

"There will be times when people will make you mad, but you have to remain calm so that you can think clearly. After you think, you may still want to 'blow your top,' but even then you don't lose control. You think about what you're doing and why. When you ride the red horse, you're not doing your best thinking before you speak or act. Remember this. There are some people who will make you mad, and you shouldn't say anything to them. Ignore them. Just go ahead and do what you gotta do. Do you know why?"

"Because if I haul off and punch 'em in the mouth, then I'll get in trouble?"

Dad didn't laugh at my response. He just shook his head no. He was serious. This wasn't a joke. He was passing on pearls.

"No, you don't need to use violence. People who always want to fight to solve things, or cuss and make a lot of noise, act that way because they aren't smart enough to express themselves any other way. You're smart enough to communicate without violence. But the reason you ignore some people, even when they make you mad, is because 'to argue with a fool makes you a bigger fool.'"

This was another one of what I came to call Dad's "Streeterisms." When it came to how to deal with fools, another of Dad's Streeterisms was, "One who knows not, and knows not that he knows not, is a fool. Shun him."

I'm sure Dad didn't create all of his Streeterisms. But he is the one who passed them on to me. His mantras provided a light to guide me through the thick, black smoke that rose from my unchecked anger.

Dad was steeped in life experience. He knew that life wasn't fair and being black wasn't easy. He was raised by a single mother, born in the South, lived in Wilmington, Delaware, until he was 12 and his mother moved to Philadelphia. He grew up poor in a tough neighborhood. While in the Army he spent time in the brig and went AWOL before he learned how to make the best of being a soldier during World War II. After he was honorably discharged, he returned home to have his dream to open a tailoring shop thwarted after he completed a training program but couldn't get the money he needed. He fought battles on his job and threatened to sue the city when he was passed over for a promotion at the Philadelphia Museum of Art after he scored higher on the civil service exam than the person who was promoted. The dispute was resolved when the city offered him a job as a security officer at a Philadelphia Water Department facility located four blocks from our home. Dad provided for us, protected us, and taught us the lessons we needed to fight the battles that awaited.

Dad listened and helped me to understand more about situations that got me so fired up. He saw beyond the obvious to the more subtle agendas being played out by others. He made me think about whether or not I was being manipulated or blindly led to make a bad decision. Dad helped me explore other ways to handle situations and the people involved. He taught me how to accept things that I could not control and to be patient and wait for a better time to act. Unaware, I learned critical thinking, conflict resolution, and how to be introspective before I graduated from high school. I desperately needed these skills. There were plenty of battles ahead.

There were times when saving me from myself was a job for others in the family. When Dad wasn't around to make me disembark from the red horse, thank God he had reinforcements. Mom knew the advice Dad gave me because they talked about all of us and what was going on in our lives. Mom and Dad were sentries assigned to watch everything that went on in and around the castle, that two-story row house in the heart of North Philadelphia. They monitored from a distance every aspect of our lives and shared information regularly. I'm sure they debriefed each other when we were not within earshot. Like all teenagers, we assumed they didn't know what was going on. But they were always up to speed on the latest drama. A time came when Mom had to step forward and make me pull back the reins on the red horse that I was determined to ride.

It was 1968, the summer before 12th grade. I was 16 when my good friend Anne told me that my boyfriend, Harvey, had cheated on me the weekend before he shipped out for Vietnam. Harvey was 19 and we met just after he graduated from Ben Franklin High School. We dated exclusively after he enlisted in the Army and came home on his first leave.

It had only been about three weeks since Harvey left for Vietnam. The Sunday morning before he left home, he called me, and he called again from a phone booth when he got to the airport. We talked or just silently hung on the line listening to each other breathe, hoping he didn't run out of change. Just as the last call to board the plane was broadcasted, Harvey said, "I love you, Kat. I'm gonna miss you. See you when I get back. I'll write you as soon as I know where I'll be stationed."

When Anne told me what she heard, I went into combat mode. I had to find out exactly what happened and who knew about it. When did they find out? And if they were my friend, why didn't they tell me?

That night, alone in my room, my stomach was in knots, and my head felt like it was about to explode. I wrote Harvey a scathing letter. I told him all that I heard and that we were through. I was so angry, the pen tore through the paper twice before I finished the letter, and my handwriting was barely legible. It was after 10 p.m. when I finished writing the letter. I was determined to mail it right away. I wasn't going to sleep until I put an end to this mess.

I knew Harvey had arrived in Vietnam because I received my first letter from him earlier that week. When I got the letter, I was so glad to hear from him; I prayed for him every day. Until all this mess, I was 16 and in love. I wore Harvey's Army-issued nameplate above my heart every day. Before I left to mail the letter, I unclipped it from my blouse and threw it in the trash can next to my bed. I was firmly strapped in the saddle on the red horse and on my way to the mailbox.

A cool breeze made for a comfortable summer night, and Mom was sitting on the porch, talking to Mrs. Smith, our next-door neighbor. Mom had overheard the rumors about

Harvey. The phone rang constantly and my friends were in and out of the house, giving me the latest updates about this major drama in my life. All day Mom listened as she went about her business. She never said anything about what she heard. As all hell broke loose, like dust in the air Mom was present but unnoticed.

I bounded down the front steps, headed for the mailbox. Mom called out, "Wait a minute, wait a minute, where are you going?"

Without slowing my pace, I looked back over my shoulder. "To the mailbox, I got to mail this letter. I'll be right back."

"Kathy, you come back here. I know you're mad about what they said Harvey was doing before he left for Vietnam. But that boy is over there now fighting for his life. Before you send him a letter that might upset him, I want you to think about it. Don't do something you'll regret. Your father done told you 'think before you act.' Now go back in the house. You're not sending that letter tonight."

Her tone was stern; her eyes were trained on me like daggers. She was not going to relent no matter what I said.

I was annoyed that Mom was now all in my business. I needed to strike back. The letter burned my hand like a piece of hot coal. I sucked my teeth, let out an audible breath, and stomped back inside the house and went to my room. I threw the stuffed animals that Harvey won for me on the boardwalk in Atlantic City earlier that summer off the bed and onto the floor. I flung myself face-down on the bed and fumed.

About a half-hour later my brother, Johnny, came upstairs and turned on my bedroom light. "Hey, what are you doin' in bed? You sick or somethin'?"

"No, turn the light out and leave me alone."

Johnny came in the room and stood by the dresser. I was lying on my side facing the other end. He bent down and tried to look at my face to see if I was crying.

"You right to be mad about all this mess they talking about. But I just think it ain't right to quit him without lettin' him tell you his side. Suppose it's not true? Suppose somebody just trying to 'screw your head off'? What about that?"

I didn't say anything.

"I know you gonna do what you want to do, but Harvey ain't a bad dude. You should at least give him a chance to tell you his side. What you got to lose?"

Johnny turned off the light and left me to sort it out.

A couple of days later I rewrote the letter. I told Harvey what I heard, but I didn't break up with him. I didn't get a response within the time I thought that I should have received one. I concluded that was the end of us.

About three weeks after I sent the letter, Harvey's mother called to tell me that he had been seriously wounded in Vietnam and was in the hospital in Japan. She was crying so hard I could barely understand what she said. My heart beat fast. "Oh God, please no," was all I could say. A couple of days later I received Harvey's response to my letter. He must have written it shortly before he was wounded. It was a long letter and lifted my spirits. I was glad that I had not sent the first letter. It's a good thing that Mom snatched me off the red horse.

Similar to the advice not to ride the red horse, another of Dad's Streeterisms was, "Control your emotions, don't let your emotions control you." These admonitions often went together, though not always. Until I was able to put into action on my own what Dad taught me, there were others who cared and watched out for me. They stepped forward to put me in check and save me from myself.

6

Don't Let Anyone Build a Bridge Over Your Nose

Senior year in high school finally arrived. It was almost time to send me off to college, if I got accepted. Dad's determination to find the money to send me to college was the same determination that he showed in everything he did, from disciplining us and paying bills to playing cards. Dad said, "Scared money never wins."

When he accomplished a goal, won a hand, or bluffed out his opponent in a card game, he said, "See, the aggressor wins nine times out of ten."

He taught me to take risks, be willing to put my money where my mouth was, and to have the heart to go after what I wanted. But first, I had to make a plan and then take action. I followed his advice and tried to remember the lessons he taught me. I became more confident in my ability to handle situations and go after what I wanted, or at least thought I could get.

I guess it was inevitable that the time would come when I attempted to outsmart Dad. That's when he taught me another Streeterism: "Don't let anyone build a bridge over your nose." This means don't let anyone try and convince you of the validity of their position or force you to make a decision, either by keeping necessary facts from you or causing you to ignore information that should be considered. The reason people do this is to get you to do what they want you to do. In order to succeed, they must distract you from seeing information that's right under your nose.

I heard Dad tell Mom about a conversation he had with some men at the corner barbershop who questioned him about why he was so determined to send me to college. The men asked Dad, "Man, do you know how much it's gonna cost you to send that girl to college and for her to live on campus?"

"I don't care. If my family has to eat beans, my daughter is going to college," Dad told them.

Some of the regulars who hung out at the barbershop tried to convince Dad that it was a waste of money to send a girl to college. "All girls go to college for is to find a husband, or they go and end up gettin' pregnant."

"Yeah, maybe that's true for your daughters, but we'll see. My daughter is going to college."

I was the first person in my family to have a realistic shot to go to college. I never told anyone that I was a little afraid of leaving the security and familiarity of home, my friends, and the neighborhood. My best friend, Carol, lived a few houses away with her aunt, uncle, and grandmother until her family moved to West Philadelphia. We had been friends since second grade. Carol and I went to different high schools; we were good students and applied to the same colleges. We wanted to go to the same college and be roommates. I was on the honor roll every year since 10th grade, co-captain of the debate team, and involved in many other school activities. Dad planned, saved, and prayed that I would go to college and live on campus because that's what I wanted.

Carol and I were accepted at Lincoln University, a historically black university located not too far outside of Philadelphia; it was all-male until the mid-1960s. We heard that Lincoln's male-to-female ratio was six to one, which was another important factor in our desire to go there. Lincoln didn't offer me much financial aid, so my parents were going to have to make a lot of sacrifices to send me there. After I was accepted at several colleges, I got excited about going away to school and especially to Lincoln. Carol and I picked out matching bedspreads, wall posters, and decorations for our dorm room. Every day we talked about going to Lincoln in the fall of 1969.

In mid-April, I received a letter from the University of Pennsylvania.

* * *

I didn't want to apply to the University of Pennsylvania because I didn't think I would be accepted. I had been accepted at many schools and it felt good. I didn't want to be rejected by Penn. My high school guidance counselor, Dr. Mozelle McKay, took her job seriously. She worked every angle to get me and all the seniors assigned to her into as many colleges as possible. She asked colleges to waive application fees because our families could not afford to pay for the many college applications she made us submit. She made us write and rewrite college essays and go on college tours. She made sure our teachers wrote recommendations and turned them in on time. Dr. McKay didn't play around. My application packages were completed and submitted before the deadlines.

She was the one who suggested that I apply to the University of Pennsylvania. I kept putting off completing the application. One afternoon I stopped by her office just to talk about the applications that I had submitted. Her enthusiasm was contagious, and I was excited. I believed her when she said, "You are going to college, young lady, and a good one at that. Believe what I tell you." That afternoon she asked, "Kathy, where is your application to the University of Pennsylvania?" She was looking through her folder that contained my file. "We need to get that in."

"Aw, Mrs. McKay, why should I apply there? I probably won't get in. You know that's the Ivy League."

Dr. McKay got up from her desk, which was piled high with folders for all the students she was trying to get into colleges, and without taking her eyes off of me, she firmly closed the door to her office. I was standing next to her desk. She walked up to me, her face close to mine, and in a stern, audible whisper from between clenched teeth, she said, "Young lady, in life don't you ever write yourself off by not going after something you want or deserve to have. You apply to that Ivy League university. You go after it. Do you hear me? If you don't get accepted, then it will be their loss, not yours. If you don't even apply, you will deny yourself for lack of trying. They won't have to deny you because you will deny yourself. Do you understand what I'm telling you?"

When I came into her office that afternoon, I was at ease and feeling good about the college acceptances that she had helped me to get. Now I stiffened. The smile I had when I came in was gone. I held my head up and looked in her eyes.

"Yes, ma'am. I'll bring the application in tomorrow morning."

Dr. McKay didn't physically shake me, but I was shaken by what she said. Her advice has never left me.

* * *

The day the letter arrived from the University of Pennsylvania, Dad was sitting on the front porch when the mailman came. He brought the letter upstairs and handed it to me. I was in my bedroom; Carol and I had just gotten off the telephone, talking about our never-ending plans for what we were going to do when we got to Lincoln. I opened the letter and read it to myself. I was accepted into the freshman class at the University of Pennsylvania, fall of 1969, and awarded a full four-year scholarship which included tuition, room, and board. The annual amount of my financial aid package was half as much as Mom and Dad earned in a year. As I read the letter, I showed no emotion. I knew it was an impressive acceptance, and a full ride was definitely a great financial aid package. But Carol and I had decided we were going to Lincoln.

Dad stood in the doorway and waited for me to tell him what was in the letter. Without a word, I stuffed the letter back in the envelope.

"What did the letter say?"

Off-handedly and with few details, I told him I was accepted and they gave me a scholarship. His eyes widened and he grabbed the letter from me.

"What? Let me see it."

Dad read the letter and began to smile. His smile got bigger the more he read. When he got to the end of the letter, he almost shouted, "Hot damn!"

With the letter in hand, he turned and left my room. Before he went downstairs, he stopped and read the financial aid part again. I stood in the hallway and watched him. I thought, *I'd better say something before he gets too happy*. In a decisive tone I said, "I'm not going to Penn. I'm going to Lincoln."

Dad halted on the steps, spun around, and looked up at me as if he couldn't believe what I said. He squinted and shook his head. By now he was looking at me as if I had lost my mind and was speaking in tongues.

"Do you understand what this letter says? Do you know how much money that school is going to give you? Lincoln is not offering to give you this kind of money. Why don't you want to go to Penn?"

I took a deep breath. Okay, this was my chance to build a bridge over Dad's nose. First, I mounted the red horse, to show Dad I was upset too. By now Dad had raised his voice as he tried to make sense out of what I said. I couldn't tell him that a primary reason for wanting to go to Lincoln was the male-to-female ratio or that I wanted to attend a historically black university. I didn't think that would convince him, especially since Penn was offering me a full ride and Lincoln was not. After what Dr. McKay said to me, I would never again express any fear about not making the grade at Penn. In response to his question I said, "Carol and I have made plans. Remember, you said that I could go to any college I wanted to, if I got accepted."

There, I did it, confronted him with his own words. I knew he wouldn't go back on his word. Dad always said that a man was as good as his word. I wasn't crazy enough to say that to him, but he got the point. I had built the bridge. He stood still in the stairwell and glared at me as I stood at the top of the steps. I thought, *What can he say now, except that I can go to Lincoln.*

After what seemed like a very long time, Dad tilted his head slightly to the side, twisted his mouth as he did when he was disgusted, and pointed his finger up the stairs at me. In a calm, firm, chilling tone that let me know he didn't want to hear any more of my nonsense, he said, "That's right, I did say that. Now you make sure you want to go to the University of Pennsylvania." He squeezed the letter tight in his hand, turned his back, and went downstairs and out the front door.

It must have been predestined. Later that week Carol was also accepted at the University of Pennsylvania. We were roommates freshman year.

My effort to attack Dad's integrity in order to achieve my objective without giving any logical reason did not succeed. I failed to build a bridge over his nose because Dad was secure in himself and never doubted his integrity. He was well aware that it was his responsibility to act not only in my best interest but in the best interest of our family. He was not about to allow his 16-year-old daughter to build a bridge over his nose.

It wasn't long before I had to find these qualities in myself.

* * *

I was a freshman at the University of Pennsylvania. It was

my first weekend on campus, and there was a big party with college students from all over the city. A guy from a small college asked me to dance, and I danced with him a couple of times. When he kept asking me to dance, I finally said no and went to the other side of the room. At the end of the party, he came over and asked if I lived in Hill Hall, which was the freshman girls' dormitory. I didn't answer. He said, "You and your girls leavin' now?"

I looked quickly around the room to give the impression that I was in a hurry or that there was someone waiting for me. "Yeah, I'll see you around."

Before I could move away, he grabbed my arm. "Let me get your phone number, maybe I can call you."

I was stunned. I knew how I would have handled this guy if he grabbed me when I was at a party in my neighborhood. But this was my first college party with all these new people. I wanted to act friendly, not stuck-up or tough, but I didn't want to give him my phone number. I sure didn't like him grabbing me. I had absolutely no interest in talking to him or ever seeing again.

I smiled and tried to sound friendly. "No, but I'm sure I'll see you around sometime."

I turned to walk away and he lit into me, not in anger but with an unmistakable disdain. "I get it, sister, you up here at this Ivy League university, so you don't have time for us poor regular brothers at the small city colleges. I bet if I was one of these Ivy League guys, you would give me your number."

The bridge was built. I knew that wasn't true. It wasn't the school he went to, I just wasn't interested in him. But I didn't want anyone to think that I was somebody who would put a guy down because he didn't go to Penn. The voice inside my head screamed, *Don't fall for that bull!* I didn't listen and gave him my telephone number.

I should have remembered the lesson Dad taught me. Instead I became defensive. I was from North Philly and militant. I wasn't some uppity Ivy League girl. I respected people no matter where they went to school or where they lived. I certainly did not think I was better than poor people. Damn it, I was poor. To prove him wrong, I gave him my telephone number. The bridge he built stopped me from seeing that I didn't need to prove myself to him.

The next two weeks were pure hell. He called my room every other day. A few times my roommate lied and told him I wasn't there and not expected until late. He just called back. Twice, uninvited, he showed up at the dormitory and pleaded with me to come to the lobby and talk to him. The first time, I went and talked with him for a few minutes. I quickly tried to get rid of him before anybody saw me. I had work to do and I was not interested in this guy on any level.

The second time he popped up, called my room, and pleaded with me to come to the lobby to talk to him. He whispered in a husky voice which I guess he thought sounded sexy, "Hey, how ya doin'? I'm in the lobby, why don't you come and talk to me for a bit?"

My skin crawled at the sound of his voice. I was studying when he called. "No, I'm busy, I got work to do."

"Aw, come on, just a few minutes." Then he attempted to reinforce the bridge. "I bet if I was one of these Ivy League guys, you'd find a little time for me, huh?"

"Just a minute, I'll be right there."

I went to the lobby, looked around, and didn't see him. Some students were standing around talking. One of them called out, "Yo, K. Streeter, some guy was looking for you. He went upstairs to the lounge."

I thought, *Upstairs to the lounge? Oh, he's making himself right at home.*

My anger erupted. I ran up the steps, two at a time. I flung the large glass door to the lounge open so hard, it hit the wall with a loud bang. He stood up slowly with a sly grin and walked toward me. I said, "Hey, look, don't call me and don't come see me anymore. I don't want to talk to you."

He stood up straight, less than a foot away. He towered

over me. He sneered, just like that night at the party, and nodded his head slowly. "Yeah, yeah, I get it; you're too good for me—"

Before he could finish whatever he was about to say, "If that's what you want to think, fine. Don't call and don't come back here to see me. You got that?"

Before he could say anything, I turned around, flung the door open as hard as when I came in, and left the room. As I bounded down the steps to the lobby, everyone looked up at me. I guess they heard me. I didn't care. That bridge collapsed.

I learned that Dad's lessons would only help me when I had sense enough to use them.

Simon Gratz High School Graduate - Valedictorian

Dad in a white shirt. He always wore a white shirt when he had to take care of business or on special occasions.

John and Margaret Streeter, sentries ...around that two-story row house in the heart of North Philadelphia.

PART II

CARRIED THROUGH

7

Take Flight

It was 1969, my freshman year at this Ivy League university. The fragile tinder box of civil disobedience was ignited every day by some new incident that happened on campus, in the city, or anywhere else. On May 4, 1970, the Ohio National Guard killed four students and wounded nine others at Kent State University in Ohio during a protest of the Vietnam War. College campuses across the nation were in an uproar. It was spring; bright-colored flowers were in bloom along the campus walks, and dark-green ivy grew thick and covered the walls of historic buildings on campus. Penn, one of the oldest universities in the nation, was surrounded with the beauty of spring as the earth awakened after winter. But Penn, like other colleges throughout the United States, was on the brink of a conflagration that might cause it to implode.

It was a bright, sunny day, and news spread fast throughout the campus that students who wanted to leave campus could take their final exams at home. Students who wanted to take exams in class were told to see their professors to make arrangements. Almost everyone wanted to leave campus as quickly as possible. Some students hurried to get away so that they could think about what happened. Some wanted to react to the Kent State massacre. I think all of us just wanted to try and get a grip and prepare for whatever was going to happen next. "Ohio," sung by Cosby, Stills, Nash, and Young, described the turmoil that raged and brought an end to my freshman year.

I landed on campus in September, a minority in more ways than I wanted to think about. I was a 17-year-old black girl, from a family with a household income of less than $10,000 per year to support a family of seven, and a graduate of a public high school that was not considered academically proficient. To tell the truth, my high school was not comparable in any way to the schools from which most of the freshman class at Penn graduated. It felt as if Mom and Dad were standing on the shore and sending me out to sea. The sea was the University of Pennsylvania, and ready or not, I was here to compete with the well-prepared and the privileged.

College was my first real foray outside the fishbowl of my neighborhood. The course that led me to college was charted after I saw four white men break down our next-door neighbor's front door when I was six years old. In elementary school, after I told Dad that I wanted to be a lawyer when I grew up and reported back to him what I had to do to become a lawyer, he and Mom set their sights on helping me to reach my goal. It wasn't until the steel-grey footlocker was packed with new sheets, towels, and all the things Mom thought I needed that it struck me, like ice-cold water poured down my back: to pursue my goal, I had to leave home, friends, and all things familiar. Going to Penn was much more traumatic than going to a junior high school outside my neighborhood, because in junior high school I came home every day and saw my family and friends.

Earlier in the afternoon, as Dad packed the car, neighbors came out on their porches and waved good-bye and yelled, "Good luck, see you soon." I was only going from North Philadelphia to West Philadelphia, but it felt like I was going to Chicago. Never in my life had I been to the section of the city where Penn's campus was located. I was assigned a room in Hill Hall, the freshman girls' dormitory, suite IV-A. Mom made my bed and helped me put my stuff away. She patted my bed pillow again. She ran her hand over the bedspread and patted the pillow every time she looked around the room, making her final checks, and then she hugged me tight. "Come on, Margaret," Dad said. He opened the door for Mom. "Kathy, you got everything? We'll call you later." They left me in my new, stark-white room with twin beds, two desks, and two closets. I was alone, surrounded by all things unfamiliar.

I didn't know anybody at Penn except my best friend and roommate, Carol. Carol lived in West Philadelphia and had come by the room earlier that afternoon and dropped off her things. It was rumored that Penn admitted 150 black students in the freshman class. Many of them graduated from West Philadelphia High School with Carol and attended a six-week pre-freshman orientation program that Penn sponsored during the summer. Carol called me when she received information from Penn about the pre-freshman program and asked if I was going. I told her no, I wasn't invited to participate. When she called, I didn't think much about it and I really didn't want to go to school during my last summer before college anyway. I felt differently when I arrived on campus and found out that students in the program took a class during the summer and earned a college credit. What I really missed was that I did not get to meet other incoming freshmen who were in the summer program. They lived on campus, learned their way around, went to parties, and formed their social networks. I didn't get to do any of that. I was an outsider.

Never mind that I didn't want to go to school during the summer, I didn't try to get into the program after Carol told me about it. Now I was suffering the consequences. I wanted to know why I wasn't invited to participate in the pre-freshman orientation program. Yeah, I went along with the decision that excluded me, but why was that decision made in the first place? I heard from some students that an administrative staff person told them that the program was for "socially and economically deprived students." Black students did not like this characterization. Also, this stereotype attached to all black students in the freshman class, even those who didn't participate in the program. Most white students, if they were aware of the program, assumed that all black students participated in it. I didn't consider myself "socially deprived" in comparison to anyone at Penn, white or black, even though the exact meaning of the term "socially deprived" was never explained to me by anyone. I acknowledged that based on my family's financial status, when compared to the students at Penn, I was "economically deprived." So why wasn't I invited to participate in the program? I asked someone in the dean's office of the College for Women, but I never got an answer. I concluded that I was not invited to participate in the pre-freshman program because Penn had written me off from the very beginning. They didn't expect me to make it through freshman year, so why waste money for me to participate in the program. That made me angry. But I remembered what Dad told me: "Think before you act. Control your emotions, don't let your emotions control you. Don't ride the red horse."

It was 1969. As a result of civil rights marches, the assassination of Reverend Dr. Martin Luther King, Jr., and race riots, predominantly white colleges and universities opened their doors and admitted black students in record numbers. Affirmative action was the key that unlocked doors. Even at age 17, I had doubts. Was affirmative action intended to have positive results or was it just an experiment? Was the purpose of affirmative action to affirm a self-fulfilling prophecy about racial inequality? Were black students admitted just to placate those who demanded equal opportunity and education? While affirmative action opened the doors to predominantly white universities in order to let black students in, there was no guarantee that we would graduate. Affirmative action did not come with a moving sidewalk to get us to graduation. I learned that there were no affirmative action curriculums, exams, or papers. The door to graduation was only opened to those who earned the right to go through it.

Now, looking back, I wonder if I was sent ahead to test the validity of the *Mismatch Theory*[1] that would be advanced—years later. My experience as a direct beneficiary of affirmative action clearly undermines the validity of the Mismatch Theory.

Penn had general requirements for all students: three natural sciences courses was one of the general requirements needed to graduate. To satisfy the natural science requirement, I took two psychology courses, but I was determined not to take any laboratory science courses or math courses. Introductory math courses required students to use the computer lab and learn various programs and logarithms. I told my suitemates, as we looked over the course catalogue to select courses for the next semester, that my best rhythms were dance rhythms, so I planned to stay away from math courses. They laughed and we continued to search for courses to meet the requirements.

What I didn't share with them or anyone else was that in the 11th grade, I promised my math teacher that I would never take math again after the difficulty I had with Algebra II. I did well in class and when the teacher tested me individually, but I made simple mistakes on tests he gave in class. After the final exam he tested me individually and compared my answers. I did much better when he tested me individually. He said he knew I understood the work, but for some reason I made simple mistakes on the final exam. He based my grade on the individual tests, my classwork, and

---

[1] Richard H. Sander and Stuart Taylor, Jr., *Mismatch: How Affirmative Action Hurts Students It's Intended To Help And Why Universities Won't Admit It.* (New York, Basic Books, 2012).

homework. He asked me to promise never to take a math class again. We laughed and I promised that I would never take math again. He may have been joking but I wasn't.

I decided to take an astronomy course, pass/fail, to fulfill the natural science requirement. It was held in a large lecture hall at 8:00 in the morning, and I don't remember any other black students taking the class. When I told my classmates that I was taking astronomy, they laughed and one of them said, "You probably thought you signed up for astrology, didn't you?"

On the first day of class, the professor announced that there would be two hourly exams and a final exam. The two hourly exams counted for half of the grade and the final counted for the other half. After the second hourly exam, my average was about a "C," so I went to see the professor to ask for extra credit work. I thought that if I earned some extra credit, I would have a cushion, just in case I didn't do well on the final exam. Unlike at my high school, there was no expectation based on my past performance that I would do well. I missed that. The professor was a slender, tall white man who wore thick, dark-rimmed glasses and was always very serious. He rarely smiled in class, and I never saw him laugh, even when talking to students after class. It was obvious that he thought astronomy was interesting and useful. I did not share his sentiments. After I asked him for extra credit work, he asked what grades I got on the hourly exams. I told him. He asked if I attended class regularly and kept up with the assigned reading. I answered, "Yes," which was partially true. I did go to every class, but the reading assignments put me to sleep.

In response to my request for extra credit work the professor said, "Well, you must understand something about the material, since you have earned a passing grade up to this point. I don't think you should expect to do any extra credit work if you're having difficulty with the regular work. Young lady, you are in the big university now. Here you will sink or swim. There will not be any extra credit."

I quietly closed the door behind me as I left his office and slowly walked through the hall and down the steps that led outside. The palms of my hands had begun to sweat. I took a long, deep breath. It was a damp, overcast day and reflected the gloom I felt—cool, no warmth in the air. Now what? I had to pass this class. From that day on, I stopped reading lying across the bed, sat at my desk, turned the music off, and stayed awake. I read the assignments, attended the classes, and passed the final exam. The professor was right. I was in the big university, and now I knew I could swim.

College was freedom. I was free to run, experiment, speak out, learn, adjust, or self-destruct. It was as if I was standing in the center of a large wheel where each spoke represented a path for me to choose and each path led into the world. My choices would determine where and how I entered the world after college. No longer under the watchful eye of Mom and Dad, I drank wine and partied until the wee hours of the morning. Once, on a school night, I went with some classmates and an upperclassman, who owned a car, to Manhattan. The discotheques stayed open all night, and we didn't get back to campus until almost 7:00 the next morning. My fellow partygoers headed to bed. I got something to eat and went to my 9:00 class. I took notes and willed my eyes to stay open and my sleep-deprived brain to focus. Here I was, doing it again, just like in high school when I wanted to do the things that the "in crowd" did. But I knew my grades better not suffer because of it. Trying to run on both sides of the fence took too much energy. I knew I had to take care of business if I wanted to graduate.

I was very active in the black students organization, Students for an Afro-American Society (SAAS), attended meetings and participated in protest marches. The atmosphere on campus was electric and always fully charged. Student unrest and outrage with the status quo in race relations and the Vietnam War was palpable. Groups such as Student Nonviolent Coordinating Committee (SNCC),

Weatherman, Students for a Democratic Society (SDS), and the Black Panther Party were raising hell and challenging authority. Gil Scott Heron's song entitled "The Revolution Will Not Be Televised" captured the sense of urgency and railed against complacency. Messages were communicated through music, the media, and rhetoric. Not only in speeches but in conversation, we called for "power to the people" and challenged one another to take action. "If you are not a part of the solution, you are a part of the problem" was a frequent, in-your-face reminder to anyone who wanted to stay on the sidelines. And in the words of assassinated leader Malcom X, the constant demand for freedom, equality, and justice was "by any means necessary." The drumbeat of discord permeated black and white students.

Every time Dad heard or read about black student protests at Penn, he called my room. He had talked with me enough to know if there was a civil rights protest, I would be in the midst of it, if possible. He usually started his conversations with me in a calm voice. After I responded to his questions about what was going on at Penn, that's when he began to shout. During one of the protests, black students marched on College Hall demanding more African American history courses and black professors. Word spread that there was a mock United Nations Conference being held at the University of Pennsylvania Museum, and the protesters marched to the museum. The news media arrived shortly after the protesters stormed into the auditorium where the conference was going on. When the TV cameras came in the room, I quickly slid from the front to the back of the crowd and went out the nearest exit. I ran back to my room at Hill Hall, which was about three-and-a-half blocks away.

As I opened the door to the suite, one on the girls who lived on my floor was on the telephone, which was on the wall in the middle of the corridor. "Oh, here she is. Kathy, it's for you. I knocked on your room door and no one answered, I didn't think you were here." She whispered as she handed me the phone and covered the mouthpiece, "It's your father."

I took the phone from her and kept my hand over the mouthpiece. Still out of breath, I tried to stop panting. "Hi, Dad."

"Hi, what're you doing?"

"Nothing."

"Look, I see on TV what's going on out there. They're protesting!" He was shouting. "You better not get involved in that mess going on. You know what you're at that school for—to get an education. Don't get mixed up in that foolishness. You can do more after you get an education. You hear me! If you get your butt put out of that school, you're coming home and gettin' a job. I don't care if you gotta go work as a waitress in Horn and Hardart [a well-known automated restaurant chain in the city]. And you gonna pay rent to live here. You understand me!"

Dad and I frequently disagreed about how to respond to social injustice. He should not have been surprised that I had strong opinions and was outspoken. I learned to stand up for what I believed to be right from watching and listening to him. He was at the March on Washington in 1963 and was a member of the NAACP. When I was growing up, he gave me *Ebony* magazines that I cut up to make a scrapbook showing dogs attacking and fire hoses turned on civil rights marchers in the South. His opinions about racism and injustice were no secret. I knew Dad was concerned for my safety and didn't want me to jeopardize my education. He also believed that I should leave this kind of fighting to men. He never said that, but just like he knew me, I knew him too.

I rolled my eyes, held the phone away from my ear, and replied, "Yes, yes, all right." It was no sense in arguing with him.

8

Beware of Ghosts

Getting adjusted at Penn was a roller-coaster ride. Just when it seemed like I had found my groove and was on track to get done what I came there for, I was confronted with another obstacle that threatened to pull me down.

Freshman year the teaching assistant for my sociology course asked to see me to go over my midterm paper. She was a young, white, female graduate student. She asked me to meet her in the downstairs lounge in Houston Hall, a building that contained classrooms and lounges where students hung out. I got there before she arrived and sat at a small table in the back of the large lounge near a stained-glass window, away from the other students. I didn't want anyone close enough to hear us. As usual the room was filled with students, and sunlight drenched the room. I recognized the teaching assistant when she came into the lounge. During the semester she came to a few of the sociology lectures, and she talked to the professor after class. It was 1969; she dressed in that "hippie look" like many students on campus. She wore torn jeans and a wool sweater that was too big for her plump body, her hair was brownish and scraggly, and she wore thick, big round glasses. She looked around, spotted me seated by the window, came over, smiled, introduced herself, and sat down.

I sat across from her, dressed in my "militant look": bell-bottom blue denim jeans, a navy peacoat, and a red, black, and green knit hat. (The hat was my first attempt at knitting, which was obvious from its odd shape.) The hat was pulled down over my large afro hairstyle and sat lopsided on my head. She thanked me for coming, pulled my midterm paper from her canvas book bag, and began going over it with me. She said that she could tell that I had read the material and understood the assignment but my writing was "horrible." She handed the paper to me. It was covered with red marks she'd made on it. She said that she did not point out all the mistakes because there were just too many, and that's why she asked me to meet with her. I sensed that this meeting was almost as uncomfortable for her as it was for me. I felt as if she was trying to give some advice to help me get a good grade in the course. I kept my eyes on the paper and my body stiffened. It was as if I was back in junior high school again.

* * *

I thought I'd escaped the ghost of Mrs. Heidle, but she was always able to find me.

You can't write! That's what Mrs. Heidle, my 7th grade English teacher, told me. I was 11 years old. She said it loud enough for everyone in the class to hear as she stabbed at my paper with her red pen. I kept my eyes on my paper as I felt the rush of perspiration under my arms. I hoped no one noticed my wet blouse. I quickly looked around to see who was watching, listening to her stomp on my spirit as if it were a cigarette butt. She attacked my paper with venom reserved for a hated enemy.

This was the junior high school I was sent to for a better education than my parents and elementary school teachers thought I could get at the neighborhood school. I don't remember what I did to warrant her taking off on me like that. I wasn't the only student called to her desk, and I don't remember what she said to them. Perhaps she was frustrated that some of the students in our class didn't get what she thought she taught us. Perhaps she hoped that she could embarrass me into doing better. I didn't tell my parents or anyone about that incident.

After Mrs. Hiedle's flogging, I carried my used, well-worn, brown hardback Warner's English book as if it was the Bible. From that day until I graduated from junior high school, whenever I did my homework or wrote anything for class, I stuck to the basics. I referred to that English book before I dared write anything that would be considered advanced. I avoided compound sentences, adverbs, or adjectives. And I rarely attempted to share my thoughts or be creative. My writing was reduced to nothing but required facts, stated as simply as possible. No more perspiration-ruined blouses for me. I don't know if Mrs. Hiedle's evaluation of my homework was intended to destroy my ability to write. But I internalized the words "you can't write." I became the pallbearer of my ability to write.

My back-to-basics approach worked pretty well, and I received good grades in my other classes. When I got to high school, I forgot about what Mrs. Heidle said to me, and I used all that I learned in her class and others. I wrote what I wanted to say and how I wanted to say it. I received some red marks for grammar and punctuation mistakes from some of my teachers in high school, but more compliments on content. But the shaming I received from Mrs. Heidle was always just below the surface.

* * *

Now a freshman at Penn, I regretted leaving that used English book at home. Was this teaching assistant the "demon spawn" of Mrs. Heidle? I didn't challenge her; I just listened. She asked where I went to high school. When I told her I went to public school in Philadelphia, she raised her eyebrows, nodded her head, and looked down at my paper. Without a word, her expression said it all. Then she asked, "What's your major?"

"Sociology."

She slowly let out a deep sigh because that was her major.

"If you want to pass the final exam or plan to major in sociology, you need to improve your writing," she whispered in a matter-of-fact tone of voice.

I nodded and kept my eyes on the marks she had made on my paper.

Later that week I took the bus and went back to my high school to see my 12th grade English teacher. I told her what the teaching assistant said and watched her closely before I asked her, "Can I write?"

She fidgeted in her chair, and the expression on her face changed from sadness to disgust. "Kathy, you probably don't write as well as a lot of the students at the University of Pennsylvania, but you can write well enough."

"What does that mean? How did I get an 'A' in English if I can't write?"

Her eyes filled with tears as she took a deep breath. "Kathy, you write pretty well. Your writing and work in class was much better than most of the students. You earned an 'A.' Now, the students at Penn probably had more intensive writing courses at their high schools than we have here. It's to be expected that they may write better than you. Here, you were one of the best. I'm sure with practice you'll do all right at Penn."

As I left her office, I boiled all that she said down to this: I can't write.

Exposed, I planned to go back to basics. I remembered that in junior high school, I understood English better after I took French. My French teacher in junior high school understood that I didn't know how to write or speak French, but unlike Mrs. Heidle, she didn't lose patience and willingly accepted the challenge to teach me. Now that I think about it, that was her job and Mrs. Hiedle's too. It was my job to learn from my mistakes and do my best to write better.

* * *

After meeting with the teaching assistant, I made an effort to write better. I never had any other complaints about my writing in college or law school. But I continued to have bouts of writing paralysis, and when it struck, my thoughts were trapped and I couldn't write anything except simple, stilted, and boring sentences.

9

The World Expands

Before the end of first semester freshman year, my roommate and best friend, Carol, pleaded with me to go to a rush party sponsored by Alpha Kappa Alpha Sorority Inc., AKA. I didn't know much about sororities and fraternities. I thought they were pretty much the same thing as the social clubs we had in high school, except on the college level. I tried to beg off. I was too militant for that stuff. Carol persisted and so I went to the rush party with her. It was held on a Sunday afternoon in late fall on Drexel University's campus, which was adjacent to Penn. About seven or eight girls interested in joining the sorority gathered in a small lounge in the Drexel Activity Center. The tablecloths, napkins, and decorations were all pink and green, the sorority's colors, and there was punch, cookies, and favors on the table for each girl. Just like the rush parties sponsored by the white sororities, we signed up in advance to attend.

After I agreed to go with Carol to the AKA rush party, I became curious about all the buzz on campus about sororities and fraternities. There were flyers posted everywhere, and banners hung in front of the three-story ornate Victorian houses that lined the campus walks and surrounding streets. These were the houses for the white sororities and fraternities. Black sororities and fraternities, even the ones chartered at

Penn, did not have houses on campus. I signed up to attend teas sponsored by two white sororities. I asked Carol to go with me but she said no. AKA was the only sorority she was interested in. I wasn't interested in joining a white sorority, or any sorority, for that matter; I just wanted to know what they were about. So, I went to both teas by myself.

Both sororities held their teas in their house, one of the large Victorian houses on campus. I had never been inside houses like these before. The white sororities served a variety of hors d'oeuvres, cookies, little cakes called *petit fours*, wine, and punch. I noticed the shocked looks on the faces of the girls when I showed up with my large afro hairstyle, which was not perfectly coifed. I wore a short, pleated skirt, white blouse, stockings, and high heels that matched the color of my pocketbook (precursor to the handbag). Since I didn't own any gold jewelry or pearls like the other girls there, I wore my usual costume jewelry, which consisted of big hoop gold-colored earrings and a long chain necklace. The food was delicious, much better than the mystery meat served in the cafeteria.

I approached members of the sorority and tried to ask questions about what was required to join. Only a few of the girls at the tea dared talk to me. The members who answered my questions were very polite but intentionally vague when they explained the process to me. Ultimately, I understood that after the rush party, if the sorority was interested in having me join their pledge club, I would receive a bid. After these brief conversations, I ate more of the delicious hors d'oeuvres, drank more wine, and took a few cookies with me before I left. At the end of the campus rush period, I was very surprised when one of the white sororities offered me a bid.

I got a kick out of showing up at places where I wasn't expected, and in some cases, not wanted. In such situations, some people made it clear, by their sideways glances, no greeting, and certainly no conversation, that my presence wasn't welcomed. One thing was certain: I was not invisible, but I could tell that some girls wished that I would disappear. Occasionally one of the sorority members or a guest would break ranks with the other girls, speak to me, and ask where I lived and where I went to high school. Sometimes they just asked straight out, why was I there? That's when I learned that when someone thinks they have a right to question me, if I choose to answer, then I have a right to question them. I enjoyed the surprised expressions, raised eyebrows, and flushed red faces, followed by an abrupt escape, when I asked them the exact same questions they had just asked me.

AKA's rush party was similar to the white sororities' teas. The AKA chapter was chartered at Penn and it was the city chapter. Black girls from Penn and other colleges in the city and small suburban schools were members. The sorors—that's what they called themselves—were very friendly and told prospective pledges about the sorority's history and the requirements to pledge. AKA was the oldest national and international sorority of black women; it was founded in 1908 at Howard University, a historically black college. After the rush I understood that AKA was much more than a social club. The members were involved in issues concerning equal rights for blacks and women, and sponsored civic, social, and cultural projects to benefit the community. Girls who wanted to pledge had to have at least a C+ average, and maintaining a good average was very important.

Carol was totally psyched. After the rush party, she really wanted to pledge. Her next-door neighbors at home were AKAs. She admired them and had wanted to pledge since she was in junior high school.

"Kathy, c'mon, pledge with me. I don't want to do it by myself. It'll be fun and we will get to meet a lot of people at other schools, especially boys." She laughed and pointed at me. "Now you know you'd like that, right?"

I was curious but not enthusiastic because I still wasn't sure that this was for me. In a tone that let Carol know I had reservations about joining a sorority, I said, "Alright, I just hope I can 'hang.' I'm not about a lot of bourgeois B.S. And you know that, right?"

"Kathy, it's not like that, you'll see. We're going to have fun."

We were accepted into AKA's pledge club along with two other girls, Irys Cottman and Annetta Byrd; they were both sophomores at Drexel University. An induction ceremony was scheduled for mid-January 1970 because by that time we would have received our grades from last semester. Our plan to pledge together fell apart when Carol didn't have the grade point average required. She asked me to pledge without her and promised that she would pledge the very next pledge season. I continued on without Carol because I didn't like quitting something once I started. Irys, Annetta, and I talked every day, several times a day, and were together every weekend. For five months we worked on projects, songs, and step routines and studied together. May 1970 we "went over," the term used when girls in the pledge group, referred to as "Ivys," successfully completed the program and were officially initiated into the sorority.

Irys and I became lifelong friends and regularly stayed in touch after she graduated from Drexel and went on to the University of Chicago for her MBA. At the end of freshman year, Carol married her high school sweetheart, who played basketball for Weber State, and moved to Utah. About a year after we went over, Annetta suddenly married some guy that none of us knew and didn't hang out with us anymore.

After I joined the sorority, my circle grew wider. I met women who graduated and were active in the sorority at the local and national levels. I attended conferences, and planned and implemented community service and cultural projects. I was elected treasurer and dean of pledges of the chapter. But it was not all business. We gave parties and traveled to other schools to attend events, where we met students from other colleges. I enjoyed meeting new people and assuming leadership positions. Carol was right: this was fun.

The more active I became in the sorority, my involvement in activities on campus decreased. I didn't completely lose touch with my friends on campus and remained active in the black students' organization, SAAS. As a result of joining AKA, I extended my reach and my grades went up. The more I had to do, the better I got at getting things done. I learned not to be afraid to venture out from home, campus, my friends, or the usual course that I was expected to follow. My world expanded and so did my confidence.

* * *

Second semester sophomore year, I frantically searched the course catalog for a class to take because a course that I had signed up for was oversubscribed. In the catalog I found a graduate course entitled "Race and the Law." It sounded very interesting and was taught by Judge A. Leon Higginbotham, Jr., on Wednesday evenings. Judge Higginbotham was a district judge on the U.S. Eastern District Court. I really wanted to take the course, but I didn't know if a sophomore would be allowed to take a graduate course. I also thought that an interesting course like this was probably full anyway. But the only way to find out was to go for it. I contacted the office for the graduate School of Social Work and was told that it was not usual for sophomores to take graduate courses, but I could take the course if the professor approved and signed a permission slip.

I called Judge Higginbotham's office and told his secretary, Mrs. Essie Brock, what I wanted. She said, "You'll need to talk to the judge. The first class is this evening; you should go and speak to him after class."

I went, approached Judge Higginbotham at the end of class, and tentatively handed him the permission slip. "Hello, Judge Higginbotham, I'm Kathryn Streeter. I called your office this afternoon to see if I could talk to you about taking this class."

The judge looked up as he hurried to put his books back in the large litigation briefcase he carried and smiled. "Yes, my secretary told me that you called. Have a seat. Why do you need special approval to take my class?" He stopped putting his books away and sat down.

"I'm a sophomore and I was told that the only way I could take a graduate course is if I got the professor's permission." I wanted to convince him that I really was interested in this course and so I kept talking.

"I read the course description, and I am interested in law because I want to be a lawyer. You may not remember but a group from my high school, Simon Gratz, came to your house one night, years ago. You talked to us about the law and what we needed to do if we were interested in going to law school. I was one of those students." Without taking a breath and as fast as I could, I tried to make my best arguments before he made a decision.

"I certainly do remember. Dr. Foster arranged for me to meet students from your high school who wanted to be lawyers. How old were you? What grade were you in?" he asked, somewhat surprised.

"I was fourteen and in the tenth grade."

"And now you're a sophomore here at Penn? That's wonderful. One of us is getting old, that's for sure."

He laughed a high-pitched laugh and his body shook. Now I felt more at ease. He remembered the visit and was pleased to see that I was in college here at Penn. At that moment I trusted him to be straight with me and give me some advice.

"I really want to take your class, but I'm just a sophomore. Do you think I should take a class with grad students?"

I wasn't disregarding the admonition that Dr. McKay, my high school guidance counselor, gave me when she warned me never to write myself off and to go after what I wanted. I wasn't writing myself off, but I needed an honest opinion from someone I could trust. Based on my experience in my astronomy class and what that professor told me, I knew I could swim at this big university, but I didn't want to get in over my head.

Judge Higginbotham said, "Kathy, the only difference between you and the graduate students in this class is that they've been in school longer. You heard me tell the students about the reading required and the final term paper for this class. If you're willing to do the work, I'm sure you'll do fine. Where do I have to sign?"

I was glad to be in the course, and I knew I had to step up my game. I attended every class, read every assignment, thoroughly researched and wrote my term paper.

Judge Higginbotham always came to class directly from court and hurriedly arrived just as the class was scheduled to begin. There was a class in the room before his, and every inch of the blackboard was covered with writing. Judge Higginbotham used the dusty board eraser to wipe away just enough of the previous scrawl to write the name of the case we were going to discuss that evening. After he repeated this routine for a few weeks, I began coming to class early and erased the blackboard before most of the students and the judge arrived.

One evening the judge's law clerk, David, arrived early just as I had finished erasing the blackboard. He said, "I noticed that the last couple weeks, the blackboard was clean before class started. Did you do that?"

"Yes, the judge is in a hurry; he doesn't have time to erase blackboards."

David looked surprised but he didn't say anything at first; he repeatedly blinked his eyes, nodded his head, and stared at me as I went to my seat. "Thanks, I'm sure the judge appreciates it."

The next week at the end of class, Judge Higginbotham thanked me.

A few weeks before the end of the semester, Dr. Ellen Goudlock, a guidance counselor from my high school, came to class. I was pleased and surprised to see her. She smiled, came over, and sat on the last row, a couple seats behind me. She told me that she and the judge were good friends and that he told her that a student from Gratz was in his class. She said when he told her I was the student, she bragged and told him that I could handle his class. Just as the judge came into room, Ms. Goudlock hurried to ask me, "Are you prepared for class?"

"Yes," I said.

I turned around in my seat and waited for the class to begin. The judge usually summarized where we left off at the end of the last class before he asked who wanted to begin the discussion about the cases we were assigned to read. I looked around the room to see who would volunteer.

This evening, after he finished his summary, the judge looked directly at me and said, "Miss Streeter, tell us about the Dred Scott case."

It felt as if someone turned the lights out. My mouth went dry and my palms began to sweat. I stuttered when I tried to speak.

The judge looked at me over his half-rim reading glasses and said, in his deep baritone voice of authority, "Come now, Miss Streeter, don't be intimidated. When was the case decided and what was it about?"

I took a deep breath, found my voice, and responded. He asked another question, I answered, and he continued to probe my thoughts about the holding in the case. Without hesitation I explained my answers. Finally, he said, "Good job," and called on someone else.

After class Ms. Goudlock sauntered over to me with a big grin on her face and said that she thought the judge was going to call on me. My head snapped back; I was shocked that I had been set up. Quickly she asked for my telephone number before she hurried out of the room and promised to call me tomorrow.

The next day she called to tell me that the judge was impressed with my analysis of the Dred Scott case, and he was very touched that I cleaned the blackboard before class. She asked, "Who told you to do that?"

"Nobody."

"He really liked that, he mentioned it to me more than once. Keep up the good work."

Before we hung up I had to ask, "Dr. Goudlock, are you coming to class next week?"

"I don't know if I'll be back next week, but I may come back before the end of the semester. Why?"

"Could you do me a favor? Please call and let me know when you're coming, okay?"

She laughed and we said good-bye.

At the end of the semester, the judge's secretary called to schedule a time for me to come to his chambers to discuss my term paper. When I arrived, the judge came out of his office and greeted me. He was glad to see me and invited me into his office. It was the first time that I had ever been in a law office, and I was very impressed to see the inside of a federal judge's chambers. There were books from ceiling to floor all around the room, a large desk, and the longest conference table I had ever seen. The view of the skyline and the clouds from the window behind his desk was picture perfect.

He pointed to one of the big leather chairs around the conference table and said, "Have a seat, Kathy. I wanted you to come in so I could tell you that you did a very good job on your term paper. I was very pleased." My paper was entitled *Slavery and the Founding Fathers.*

"I also wanted to ask if you would be interested in working for me as a research assistant." He was writing a book entitled *In the Matter of Color.*

I wanted to jump up and down as I replayed in my head what he asked me. He had just offered me a job. I'm going to work for a federal judge!

"Yes, yes, I would like that."

I never asked what were the hours, what did I have to do, or how much he was going to pay me.

I floated all the way back to campus. I couldn't wait to tell Mom and Dad. How did this happen? Was it because I followed the example of Mrs. Holmes, my fourth-grade teacher, and did something unexpected to help someone? Was it because I reached beyond the track assigned to me and went after something I wanted, like Dr. McKay told me? I didn't know why it happened, but I was so glad that it did.

Judge Higginbotham would later write my recommendations to law school.

10

Fork in the Road

Things changed. At the beginning of sophomore year, Harvey's tour of duty in the Army ended and he came home. He had been my boyfriend since 10th grade and we talked about getting married after he got out of the Army and I graduated from college. Even though I always talked about going to school to become a lawyer, I don't think Harvey ever expected me to go to law school after college. He talked about becoming a barber and opening a barbershop and that I would be a schoolteacher. When he came home on leave during my freshman year, I usually went home to see him, and a few times he came on campus to visit me. Without thinking about it, I kept my worlds separate. I had a romantic interest or two on campus during freshman year, but everyone knew I had a boyfriend in the Army.

The summer between freshman and sophomore year, Pauline, Anne, and Booty, my friends from home, got married or had children. Now when I went home, things were different. My friends had responsibilities and couldn't just jump and run like we used to. I went home less sophomore year. When I came home freshman year, I stayed the entire weekend. After I pledged the sorority, I only stayed overnight or for the afternoon, just long enough to get my bi-weekly allowance from Dad. I was in a hurry to get back to school to party with my sorority sisters or go to parties on campus with my new friends.

After Harvey was discharged from the Army, he wanted to visit me more often on campus. That's when I discovered that I preferred having an away boyfriend. When Harvey came on campus to visit, I told my friends that I couldn't hang out with them. Harvey wasn't comfortable around them. Like most of my friends from the neighborhood, Harvey had preconceived ideas about "college kids," and he wasn't interested in getting to know my college friends. Their interests were different and so were their future paths. Sometimes I told Harvey not to come on campus because I had to study. I suspected that he found ways and other girls who lived in the neighborhood to occupy his time when he wasn't with me.

Changes… Feelings slipped away; it felt like warm water after a refreshing bath going down the drain. It was too hard trying to keep things as they once were. It was sad to see tight bonds of friendships that had once meant everything to me become familiar threads. As for my relationship with Harvey, I didn't feel the same way I did in high school, and I stopped trying to convince myself that I did. Harvey and I didn't have an argument or explosive break-up. Months passed and we drifted apart. One evening he drove me back to school after I came home for one of my brief visits. We sat silently in his car in front of High Rise South, the dormitory where I lived. Several minutes passed before we just said good-bye. He looked straight ahead; I didn't ask him to come in, and he didn't attempt to kiss me before we parted. I stepped out of the car and our relationship. I walked up the steps alone and went to my apartment, where I felt at home.

Sophomore year brought about a seismic shift in the foundation that supported me before I came to college. Quietly and without words, I moved away from many of the people, places, and things that were once so warm and familiar. Not wanting to leave the past behind weighed heavy on me. The lyrics from movie *Cooley High* said it best: "And I'll take with me the memories to be my sunshine after the rain. It's so hard to say good-bye to yesterday."

* * *

It was spring 1971, the end of sophomore year. I went to a regional conference with the sorority in Annapolis, Maryland, and that's where I met Frank Kirk, a midshipman at the U.S. Naval Academy. He was 6'3" tall and played basketball. We met at a party arranged for the AKAs and midshipmen. When I saw him in his Navy midshipman dress uniform with his cap tucked under his arm, I was very impressed. *He was fine.* We danced, laughed, and talked every minute that I was not required to attend a meeting. The night before I left to come back to school, he gave me his midshipman pin. This meant we were engaged to be engaged. He had to ship out at the end of the school year for a summer detail at sea, and afterwards he was going home to California. We wouldn't see each other again until he came back to the Naval Academy in the fall. We promised to write and call each other every chance we got.

In 1971, the summer between sophomore and junior year, I stayed on campus and worked as a counselor in the pre-freshman program (the same pre-freshman program that I didn't get invited to attend my freshman year). Irys, one of my sorority sisters who lived in Washington, D.C. and went to Drexel University, didn't go home that summer. Since many of our sorority sisters lived in Philly or were home for the summer, our chapter gave a cabaret party to raise money for the projects we planned for next year.

The afternoon before the cabaret, a few sorority sisters came to my dormitory to rehearse songs and step routines that we wanted to perform at the cabaret. I intended to go home to North Philadelphia after we rehearsed to get my allowance and return to campus to get dressed before the cabaret. After the rehearsal Carly, a member of my sorority who went to Cheyney State University, offered to drive me and another sorority sister home. On the way Carly stopped by her boyfriend Michael's house. He came outside to see who was in the car, and she introduced him to us. Michael came with her to the cabaret later that night.

I saw Michael again when I went to Omega by the Sea in Atlantic City with a few of my sorority sisters. Omega by the Sea was an annual event; black college students from all over the East Coast converged on Atlantic City and partied on the beach and in nightclubs around the city all weekend. The next time I saw Michael was in the fall, on Cheyney's campus at a barn dance sponsored by Alpha Phi Alpha fraternity, which was Michael's fraternity. We spoke and danced a couple of times.

In November 1971 I saw Michael at the Kappa House after the Kappas' annual Thanksgiving cabaret. He asked me to dance and told me his name. As we began to dance I said, "Hi, I know you. You're Carly's boyfriend, we've met before." This was the first time we said much more than hi to each other.

"Oh yeah," he said nonchalantly as we danced, "but I don't go with Carly anymore."

We danced a couple of times before he asked if I wanted a ride home after the party. Initially I wasn't going home after the party because a few of us planned to spend the night at Irys' apartment. Michael was nice looking, thin to medium build, a perfectly shaped big afro and a thick black mustache. He was somewhat reserved but confident, and he seemed like a nice guy. I was curious and wanted to know more about him. I decided to let him take me home. He called the next day and asked to take me to Zechariah, a popular nightclub downtown.

I wasn't going to date Michael again, and I confided my reasons to Irys after that first date. Irys was a couple of years older than I, a senior in college, and we pledged AKA together, which made us "line sisters." She knew me pretty well and I respected her opinion. I told her I didn't date married men, guys who were engaged or had girlfriends, or guys who ever dated anyone I knew. Since Michael used to go with Carly, that meant he was out.

Irys tilted her head to one side and gave me a quizzical look before she shook her head and started to laugh so hard she almost couldn't speak. "Sister, you should just go ahead and become a nun and not date anybody. You got too many darn rules."

So I made an exception to my rule. Before Michael, the guys I considered my boyfriends were away in the military or the Naval Academy. From the beginning of our relationship, Michael visited every weekend and we talked on the phone almost every day. He always came with plans for how we would spend our time: concerts (Roberta Flack and Donny Hathaway, Curtis Mayfield, Carole King), picnics (the first Greek Picnic), parties, hanging out with friends, occasionally dinners at fancy restaurants and a trip to New York, which I didn't think he could really afford on the salary from his part-time job.

Michael majored in early childhood education and planned to go on to graduate school. He had a variety of interests: member of the editorial staff of the school newspaper, The Cheyney Record, tuba player in the school band and his fraternity. Notwithstanding the demands of his interests, he made me feel that our relationship was important to him. About a month after we began dating, Michael insisted that I sever all ties with Frank. After I agreed to return Frank's midshipman pin, Michael took me to the post office and watched me put it in the mail. Michael was industrious, sure of himself and not intimidated by my goal to become a lawyer. He gave me space and that kept us close.

Michael and I dated exclusively until I graduated in December 1972. The summer between my junior and senior years, we talked about getting married after college. One Saturday afternoon during that summer, we went to jewelers' row, located on Samson Street in Philadelphia. We walked and looked in the jewelry store windows that lined the narrow streets. We went in and out of stores, looking at engagement rings and wedding bands. After a few hours we picked out an engagement ring, and Michael put it on layaway. We talked about getting married in June of 1973. As soon as I got back to school, I called Irys and told her that Michael and I picked out an engagement ring. Most of my sorority sisters knew that Michael and I had talked about getting married, but picking out a ring made it a lot more than just talk. I never told Mom and Dad about the ring and never mentioned anything to them about marriage. I planned to tell them, just not then.

* * *

Dad didn't care too much for any of the guys I dated in college. Whenever I introduced him to any guy, he was polite, greeted them cordially, but was not interested in them becoming important in my life. Michael was down-to-earth and friendly when he met my family. He joked with my younger sisters, Ellen and Reese, and talked sports, especially about the Eagles, his favorite football team, with my older brother, Johnny. Michael didn't settle for Dad's reserved greeting; instead he engaged him. Michael told Dad about his family and that his father grew up across town. That was how people who lived west of Broad Street in Philadelphia referred to the area on the east side of Broad Street. Dad grew up across town too. When Michael mentioned his father's name, Dad was surprised that he knew Michael's father and his uncles. They grew up in the same neighborhood, and Dad went to school with Michael's Uncle Albert. With that connection, shared roots, Michael was all right. Dad's attitude toward Michael changed from cool and reserved to warm and almost welcoming. Everyone in our house was totally shocked when Dad let Michael drive his car once. Dad never let anybody drive his car. Wow!

During the summer after junior year, my sorority sisters Carol and Linda and I gave a makeup demonstration in the student lounge down the hall from our apartment. As fate would have it I had another roommate named Carol. This Carol was not the Carol from my freshman year. This Carol was my sorority sister, as was Linda. The apartment was on the 13th floor in one of three new high-rise towers on Penn's campus. We each had our own bedroom, shared a large living room with a Pullman kitchen. Carol and Linda were both from Philadelphia and we met at Penn freshman year. Our apartment was a frequent meeting place for our friends from home, fraternity and sorority members, and other students. I invited Mom to the makeup demonstration and Dad brought her. He went into my bedroom to watch TV and wait for Mom.

When I came back to the apartment to get more punch, Dad called me, "Kathy, come here."

I opened my bedroom door. Dad sat on the bed and pointed at the door. "What is that on the back of your door?"

It was a note written on a sheet of paper that Michael had taped to the back of the door. It read, *I didn't want to wake you. I'll see you later. Love, Michael.* My eyes widened; my heart skipped a beat. An unspoken *Oh shit!* caught in my throat before I gave the quickest answer I could think of. "Uh, Michael came by and I was sleep, so he left a note on the door."

Dad's eyes locked on mine and would not release me. It felt as if he was looking through me. He slowly nodded his head before he sarcastically said, "Yeah, right."

"Dad, I got to go. They're waiting for this punch."

My heart pounded as I bolted from the room and ran up the hall. I knew Dad liked Michael, but he didn't like him that much.

* * *

In the fall of 1972, Michael and I were student teaching and prepared to graduate in December. I graduated early with a Bachelor of Arts degree, a dual major in history and sociology and a certificate in secondary education. I accomplished that in three-and-a-half years instead of the usual four years. I was able to graduate early because I took extra courses during the year and a course during the summer. It felt good to graduate from Penn early, and I had better than a 3.0 grade-point average. I did pretty well for a black girl from an underachieving, overcrowded, neighborhood public school in Philadelphia who wasn't invited to the pre-freshman program for minority students. If anyone thought that it was a waste of money to offer me an opportunity to participate in the pre-freshman program, or thought that because of my background I probably wasn't going to graduate anyway, I hoped that they were happy now. I saved them more than the cost of the pre-freshman program; I saved them the cost of a semester. If it had not been for my high school counselor, Dr. McKay, I wouldn't have applied to Penn.

* * *

Everything was on track. I applied to several law schools and waited to hear from them. Just as the seasons turned, Michael became distant. Our relationship changed in the same way that the warm days of summer gradually become cooler in the fall. Leaves once bright green turned colors and dropped from the trees. Just a few months earlier we were inseparable; now Michael had things to do on campus or with his fraternity. I sensed that something was up. He had secrets and I had doubts.

As the holidays approached, one afternoon Michael met me at Judge Higginbotham's chambers before we went Christmas shopping. I introduced him to the judge and everyone in the office. I finished my last class in the middle of December and packed up my things. In the same way that he delivered me on campus freshman year, Dad arrived early in the morning, loaded my boxes into the trunk of the car, and took me back home. Mom painted my bedroom pink and all the furniture green, which were my sorority colors. The room was cheerful and bright. She looked forward to my coming back home.

Michael and I planned to go out on New Year's Eve; we saw each other the day before and spoke on the phone earlier that afternoon. On New Year's Eve Michael didn't call or show up. Pauline and Anne came by and asked if I wanted to hang out with them. Before I went away to college, on New Year's Eve the three of us would go to parties in the neighborhood, toast at every house we visited, and always brought the New Year in with laughs, excitement, and high hopes. This New Year's Eve I didn't want to go out with them. I stayed in my cheerful room and sulked.

* * *

It was January 1973. I had not heard from any of the law schools that I applied to. Because I graduated early, even if I was accepted, classes wouldn't start until the fall semester. I needed a job. The day after New Year's Day, I went for a job interview at a male youth detention center located in Bucks County, just outside the city. My cousin Carol's boyfriend, Rodger, worked there and arranged for me to be interviewed for a position as a counselor. Rodger told his supervisor that I had just graduated from Penn and was looking for a job. The interview lasted all day. Rodger's supervisor and another counselor talked to me, showed me around the building, and told me that the boys could get out of hand sometimes. They repeatedly told me that counselors had to be able to handle themselves, especially in violent situations. They watched my expression as I looked around and asked me if I thought I could handle the job. If I wanted the job, I knew what I had to say. And I told them I could handle it. They took me through a couple of housing units where the residents lived. The residents were boys who ranged in age from 14 to 18. They were sent to this institution by the courts for crimes they were found to have committed.

Some boys called to me as I walked with the supervisor and the counselor. "Hey, baby, why don't come over here, I got something for you. Hey, you got an ol' man? I bet I can show you somethin'."

The counselor yelled back, "You better keep quiet before you get locked down."

Some of the boys got angry and started cursing. Things started to heat up. My chest tightened.

While this was going on, the supervisor kept talking and explained the daily routine. As we were about to enter another unit, he stopped and quickly looked around. Six boys approached us. They came up the hall and started with the same "hey, baby" crap. I was dressed in a dark-blue pinstriped pants suit, pantyhose, and low-heeled pumps. Rodger told me to wear pants because I might go on the unit. This situation reminded me of when I was a student teacher at South Philadelphia High School. I was 20 years old, only a few years older than the students in my class. Here I was surrounded by these boys and, at age 20, I was not more than a few years older than most of them.

The supervisor looked over at me and, with an urgent whisper, like something was about to happen, he said, "You think you can handle these guys?"

Before I answered, in a harsh tone he told the boys to quiet down and stand still. I watched as they got closer to us. They became louder, strolled harder, stroked their chins, and looked me up and down.

"Yes, I think so."

My tone was more confident than I felt as the boys got within inches from me. I grew up with guys who were at least as tough as these guys, if not tougher, and more dangerous. I thought, with the supervisor here and counselors just a call away, what were they going to do to me. The supervisor grabbed a key from the large metal key ring attached to his belt and opened the door to the shower room. He pointed to four of the boys and told them to go in the room. Then he turned to me and said, "I want you to go in there with them. See if you can handle 'em."

I flashed a look at the supervisor to see if he was serious. He was. I watched the four boys go into the room. Now they were whooping and hollering and saying all kinds of stuff. "Yeah, let her come on in here. I ain't seen my girl in a while. C'mon in here, baby."

As I walked in the room, the supervisor pushed another boy, whom he had not allowed in, back outside as he tried to push his way into the room. The supervisor closed the door, and I heard the lock turn. The boys inside kept yelling, and one boy stuck his chest out and loudly asked, "What's your name? You gotta boyfriend? What you doin' here anyway?"

"My name is Miss Streeter; what's your name?"

I didn't sound as confident or at ease as I was trying to be. The tallest one of the boys walked up on me. He was at least six feet tall and skinny. He stood about six inches from me. I was five feet six inches tall and weighed 120 pounds. When he stopped in front of me, my eyes were level with his shoulders. The other boys stood behind him and watched us. Suspense sucked the air out of the room. Fear hung above my head like a heavy wool blanket waiting to cover me. I shifted from one foot to the other and instinctively backed away from the boy. I needed to see his hands and his eyes, and I didn't want to have to look up to him.

"I ain't seen my girl in a long time," he said. He spoke quietly. His eyes were dark and menacing, just like the tone of his voice. His eyes slowly roamed my body. He pursed his lips and nodded his head.

I felt almost captured. I watched him and remembered what Dad once told me: "All animals can sense fear. Never show fear because some people will take that as a sign of weakness and try to hurt you. Remember, fear is based on ignorance, not knowing. The more you know about a person, the less reason you will have to fear them. But never forget that even the lowest form of animal can feel pain."

I readjusted my footing again. I was far enough away from him in case he tried to grab me, but close enough to deliver a kick with force to his private parts. Then I asked him, "Where does your girl live? Has she been here to see you?" My matter-of-fact tone was intended to convince him that I wasn't afraid.

He looked down at the floor. "Naw, she ain't been up here yet, but my mom's gonna bring her to see me this month," he said.

Then the other boys started telling me about their girlfriends, what they looked like and how often they came to visit. I sat down on the long, wooden bench with my back against the cold, white-tiled wall. I listened and asked questions as the boys talked. They wanted to tell me their stories and what they planned to do when they got "back to the world"—that is how they referred to going home.

After about ten minutes, the supervisor unlocked the door and beckoned with his head toward the hallway. "Okay, fellas, let's go, back to the unit."

The tall boy who had walked up on me earlier had that menacing look again. He walked by me slowly as he went out the door and told the supervisor, "She a'ight."

* * *

The supervisor took me back to his office, and I asked if I could make a phone call. He stepped out of the office and I called Michael. I had not heard from him since before he stood me up on New Year's Eve.

When Michael answered the phone, I attempted to sound light and happy.

"Hey, how you doin'? I thought I would catch you home. If you didn't want to be with me on New Year's Eve, all you had to do was say so."

"It wasn't that. I went to New York with Al and—"

I interrupted. I didn't want to hear it. I continued asking questions like I gave a damn. "Did you have a good time?" I was still pissed off but wanted to sound nonchalant. I was on the red horse, but I had my emotions under control.

"It was one of the worst New Year's Eves I ever had. We went to—"

Again, I interrupted. "That's too bad, sorry to hear that. I just called to tell you that it's over. We're through. Now you can spend more time with the fellas or whoever. Maybe you'll have a better time next year. I'll see you around."

Silence. I waited for him to say something.

"Kathy…" A long pause before he said, "Never mind. I'll see you."

I hung up.

The supervisor came back into the office and asked me some more questions. The interview ended and so did my relationship with Michael.

11

Dad Guides But Children Make Their Own Decisions

When a father remains present, in every sense of the word, in the lives of his children, that doesn't ensure a positive outcome for all or even most of them.

Khalil Gibran, in his book *The Prophet*, wrote about children and captured what Mom and Dad learned to endure in raising their children:

Your children are not your children.
They are the sons and daughters of Life's longing for itself.
They come through you but not from you,
And though they are with you, yet they belong not to you.

You may give them your love but not your thoughts.
For they have their own thoughts.
You may house their bodies but not their souls,
For their souls dwell in the house of tomorrow,
which you cannot visit, not even in your dreams.
You may strive to be like them, but seek not to make them like you.
For life goes not backward nor tarries with yesterday.

You are the bows from which your children as living arrows are sent forth.

The archer sees the mark upon the path of the infinite,
and He bends you with His might that His arrows may go swift and far.
Let your bending in the archer's hand be for gladness;
For even as He loves the arrow that flies,
so He loves also the bow that is stable.

(*The Prophet* by Khalil Gibran, "On Children")

The Prophet was one of Dad's favorite books. It was included in his personal library, a collection of books he kept on the top shelf above the mantelpiece in his bedroom. Dad and Mom were strong and stable bows.

Dad taught lessons and set rules. He described himself as "a realist, practical with good common sense." When he gave us instructions, he wanted us to heed his counsel. But in his heart, he knew that we would make our own decisions and suffer the consequences or enjoy the rewards that resulted. Even when we did something that he and Mom didn't approve of, we never doubted that they loved us. After my brother, sisters, and I grew up, we made decisions that led us into uncertain and sometimes perilous situations. As we ran headfirst into uncharted or dangerous circumstances, Mom and Dad watched from a distance. When we leaned to our own understanding and did what we wanted despite their warnings or wishes, we felt their pain.

My brother, Johnny, was the first one of us to ring the bell of disappointment for Mom and Dad. Johnny was always enamored with style and being hip, down with the latest in everything. Ultimately, he learned to be a leader and not a follower, but not until he overcame a 12-year drug addiction.

Johnny was 19 years old when Dad confronted him about his drug use. Dad gave him an ultimatum: "Stop it or get out of my house." Johnny had graduated from high school and had a job. They argued loud and often. "I ain't doin' nothin'," Johnny said when Dad confronted him. "I ain't messin' with that stuff."

Dad did not graduate from high school but he read extensively, everything from the Bible, African American history, existentialism, politics, and philosophy to daily newspapers and the *Philadelphia Tribune,* the bi-weekly African American newspaper. Notwithstanding his lack of a high school diploma, Dad was most assuredly intelligent, and he had an advanced degree in life on the streets. He confronted Johnny verbally and, on more than one occasion, physically. Dad did everything within his power to redirect Johnny. His efforts failed.

Dad put Johnny out of the house. He knew from the cold stares, rolled eyes, and grumbling from everyone in the house that we did not agree with his decision. Mom never contradicted Dad in front of us. Once I heard her plead with Dad to let Johnny come back home.

"No. He is not coming back here as long as he's on that stuff. And I don't want him in this house when I'm not home."

When Dad said no, he meant it. Johnny remained out of the house, except when Mom or my younger sister Ellen left a window in the basement open for him to sneak into the house for a warm place to sleep. This was not the first time Johnny challenged Dad's rules and paid a price.

God knows Mom and Dad deserved a break. They unselfishly gave all of us their time, love, and support and stood ready to take on anyone who dared bring us harm. Now it was my turn to take their hopes into the future.

The late 1960s and the early 1970s were turbulent times. Dad strenuously advocated for civil rights but he remained very pragmatic. He constantly told all of us that education was the key to open doors and confront barriers. After I went to college, Dad and I had some very heated arguments when I spouted what he called "militant confrontational rhetoric." In the heat of our arguments, he challenged my youthful naïveté, which he called "ignorance and stupidity." Not deterred by his assessment of my ardent militancy, I challenged his old ideas as no longer relevant to the realities of what was happening at that time. Of course, I never thought and certainly never would fix my mouth to say that his ideas were stupid. This battle of wills should not have surprised him. He was the one who taught me that I had a right to express my opinion.

As graduation day approached, my dream to become a lawyer was in limbo as I awaited responses from the law schools that I applied to. There was nothing I could do but wait and it was killing me.

* * *

I was hired as a long-term substitute teacher at Strawberry Mansion Junior High School, which was in the neighborhood where I grew up. Michael and I ran into each other at parties and sometimes he drove me home. A few months after we broke up, he came by to show me the new car he bought, a 1973 silver-grey Ford Mustang Mach I, white leather interior with grey trim. It was a boss car. He knew it and couldn't wait for me to see it. Yeah, we still liked each other but it didn't matter. It was over. I was seeing other people, and I assumed that he was too. I had learned that relationships change.

My graduation from the University of Pennsylvania was scheduled to be held on Monday, May 21, 1973. Even though I graduated in December 1972, Penn's graduation ceremony was held in the spring at the end of the academic year. I was the first one in the family, including aunts, uncles, and all my first cousins, to graduate from a four-year college. Nobody was bragging but this was a big deal. Mom made preparations for a huge graduation party. The house was cleaned from top to bottom, freshly ironed and starched curtains hung from the windows in the kitchen and all the bedrooms, furniture was rearranged to accommodate all the guests she invited. The party was Sunday, the day before graduation. Mom invited everybody she could think of, including aunts, uncles, cousins, friends, neighbors, my sorority sisters, college friends, co-workers, Michael and his parents, and one of the guys I was dating. Every room was decorated; a large cake emblazoned with a congratulatory message in pink and green took up most of the buffet in the dining room. There were all kinds of food and drink and plenty of both. Music, laughter, hugs, kisses, handshakes, and well wishes filled the house.

Later Michael told me he didn't want to come to the party, but his mother insisted that he come and bring her. From the many smiles, bear hugs, loud and warm greetings he gave and received, it was obvious that he was glad he came. The old crew we hung out with when we went together hadn't seen Michael in months and was surprised to see him. The guy I was dating at the time stood off in a corner and watched as Michael and our friends reminisced about the crazy things we did in the past.

After a while Michael went to get a drink, and when he came back to his seat, he accidentally sat in a plate of food which he left on the chair. He went to the bathroom to get cleaned up. When he came back he said, "It was good seeing y'all. I got to go now, y'all take care."

I went into the hallway just outside the bedroom that Mom had arranged as a sitting room for my friends and said, "Why are you leaving so soon?"

Michael shrugged and said, "It's time for me to go."

I walked away and went into a small room that adjoined Mom and Dad's bedroom, and Michael followed. I closed the door and asked, "Why?"

Michael put his hands in his pockets, twisted his mouth, and kept his eyes on the floor. I could tell he wanted to say something. I waited.

"What difference does it make? You got your other man here. It's just time for me to go."

I started to explain but instead I went on the offensive. "Yeah, like you've been sitting home all alone after we broke up thinking about me, right?"

"Look, Kathy, I don't want to argue. Things didn't have to be like this if we had got married back when I first asked you," he said.

"Oh, it's all my fault?" I said sarcastically before I took a deep breath and retorted, "I told you that maybe we should live together for a while after we graduated."

"Look, if I'm not good enough to marry, then we don't need to live together."

I rolled my eyes and let out a loud sigh. "You want to get married? Then let's go."

There was a knock on the bedroom door. It was my cousin Carol. She handed me a large, beautifully wrapped box with an overnight bag inside. I thanked her and she went back downstairs.

"See, you just playing. I'm serious," Michael said.

"I'm serious too. Let's go."

"When, right now?"

"Yes, right now."

I grabbed the yellow flowered mini dress that I planned to wear to graduation, which was hanging on the back of the bedroom door, and stuffed it into the overnight bag. I went to my bedroom and scooped most of the gift money that I had received throughout the day from under my mattress, grabbed some underwear from my dresser drawer, put it in the overnight bag, and zipped it up. I went back to the room where Michael waited.

"Let's go," I said.

We passed Mom as we left the party. She was at the front door, laughing as she greeted more guests and welcomed them to the party. She waved good-bye to us. Michael stopped by his house and got a suit and a small suitcase. When I saw that he had a suit, I thought, *Uh-oh, he's serious.*

"Kathy, once I leave the city, I'm not bringing you back. So if you don't want to do this, say so now."

"I'm ready, let's go."

I thought that after we drove a little while, I'd ask him to take me back. He drove and we listened to the oldies that played on the radio every Sunday. The song "Ain't No Woman Like the One I Got" by the Four Tops must have played ten times as we drove from Philadelphia to Atlanta, Georgia. We arrived in Atlanta early in the morning on May 21, 1973. I asked Michael to find a telephone booth because I needed to call home. It was graduation day. The telephone rang once before Dad answered.

"Hi, Dad…"

"Where are you?"

"Atlanta, Georgia."

"Where? What are you doing there?"

"Dad, I'm going to get married—"

"Why couldn't you wait until after today? And who are you supposed to be marrying anyway?"

"I'm marrying Michael."

I don't know if he heard me because as soon as I answered him, Mom was on the telephone.

"Kathy, do you know what time it is? You've got to be at graduation by eight-thirty this morning. Where are you?"

"Mom, I'm not going to graduation. Michael and I are getting married. Mom, I need you to take my cap and gown back to school; it has to be turned in after graduation today."

"Oh, for goodness sakes." There was a long pause before she said, "All right. But why did you need to get married today?" She sighed and sounded so disappointed. "I'll see you when you get back here."

I didn't have an answer for her question. Now I wished I'd asked myself that question before I left the party.

* * *

Michael and I planned as much as we could on that 12-hour drive from Philadelphia. We intended to get married and live in Atlanta. I soon learned that all important decisions, even eloping to get married, required a lot more advance planning than that. We needed birth certificates and a marriage license. We didn't have either. We needed blood tests, which I refused to get. We didn't have wedding rings or a place to get married. Less than 48 hours after we arrived in Atlanta, we returned to Philadelphia and got birth certificates from city hall. Then we drove to Elkton, Maryland, and applied for a marriage license. I didn't need a blood test to get married in Elkton. The day before we went back to Elkton, I called Mom and told her why we came back to Philadelphia and asked if she wanted to go and be with me to get married.

"No, you go ahead. Your father thinks you're already married and that's why you didn't go to graduation. I'll see you when you get back."

She was right; Dad would have been even angrier if I missed graduation and four days later we still weren't married. I didn't tell her that I called home earlier that afternoon and my youngest sister, Reese, answered the telephone and whispered, "Kathy, you made Daddy cry."

I understood why Mom said no, but deep down I wanted her there with me. This was another consequence of not thinking before I acted.

Michael and I got married at 10:30 p.m. at the Little Wedding Chapel in Elkton, Maryland.

* * *

By the end of May 1973, I had upped the ante from anxious anticipation waiting to hear from the law schools, to an impulsive plunge into an unknown future as a married woman. I walked through each day, dazed. I appeared to be in full control, but I was in total awe of what was going to happen next.

After I eloped, the next time I saw Dad was two weeks later. It was a sunny Saturday morning in June. Michael and I had stopped by to get some more of my things. I had come home several times before, but Dad wasn't there. When we came in the house, Dad was standing in the dining room. He looked past Michael as if he wasn't there and fixed his stare on me. If I never knew what a piercing look felt like before, I knew it that day. Dad waited for me to come into the dining room to speak to him. He barely returned my greeting. Instead, he went immediately to the large breakfront china closet and removed three white business envelopes which were addressed to me.

"Here." He thrust the envelopes at me.

Each one was from a law school that I had applied to. Just a few weeks ago these letters were all I could think about. Now my mind was filled with such matters as finding a place to live, getting furniture, deciding what to call myself, to hyphenate or not to hyphenate my last name. I took a deep breath. I could tell that Dad was anxious and still angry. He stood in front of the china closet, his eyes locked on me as he waited for me to read the letters. I stood at the dining room table and read each letter to myself. I had been accepted at all of the law schools I applied to. Villanova University Law School offered me a full tuition scholarship with room and board. Suddenly it felt as if my life had been thrown into the spin-cycle and the only speeds were fast and faster.

When I finished reading, Dad asked, "What did they say?"

"I've been accepted to law school."

Dad bit his bottom lip hard. His expression flashed both anger and disappointment. A few weeks ago, this news would have made both of us ecstatic. Now, just married, facing my father and my new husband in the living room behind me, I frantically searched my mind for something to say. I wanted to make Dad feel better about all of this.

"I still plan to go to law school. I can get a deferment and go next year."

That look of disappointment never left his face. I could tell from his expression what he was thinking: *Yeah, right, who do you think you're fooling?* Every nerve in my body quivered from the pain of his disappointment. There was nothing I could say to make it right. I knew that Dad had fought hard for my dream to be a lawyer, and now look at what I'd done.

Dad nodded and continued to give me that look. After a few long, silent minutes he said, "Kathy, go upstairs. I want to talk to Michael."

I started to protest that I was married now and I didn't have to go upstairs. But his expression let me know that that was not what I should say. Without a word from me, he sensed my protest. "I'm still your daddy. Go upstairs. I want to talk to him."

My heart pounded as I climbed the steps. I thought that this was going to be the shortest marriage in history. I knew Dad wasn't a violent man, but I was a little afraid that I was about to become a widow. I tried to listen over the banister. Dad told everyone to leave the house and go outside on the porch before he took Michael into the kitchen to talk to him.

After about 30 minutes, Michael came upstairs. He was somber but not angry. I asked him what Dad said. I could tell that whatever Dad said had an impact on him.

"Your mom and dad are hurt about the way we got married. Your dad thinks that now you won't go to law school."

As always, I was ready with a response. I had to fix this. "I can get a deferment and go next year. I know people who have gotten—"

Michael shook his head no and cut me off. "You will go to law school now. I got a job and I can also work part-time at Leo's." Leo's was a men's clothing store where he used to work on the weekends before he graduated from college. "Nobody is ever going to say that you didn't become a lawyer because of me."

The Little Wedding Chapel
Elkton, MD.
Eloped, to everyone's surprise.

Newly wed.

Happily, unaware of what lay ahead.

12

I Must Own My Dream

There is a difference between owners and investors.

Summer of 1973 I accepted the offer to attend Villanova University Law School. I was anxious but more excited about going to law school. Earlier that summer, I went to see Judge Higginbotham and told him the news about my acceptances to law school and that I got married. I expected the judge to be pleased because he wrote letters of recommendation for me to all the law schools that I applied to.

When I arrived at his chambers, his secretary buzzed the intercom to let him know that I was there. The judge came out of his office and greeted me with a welcoming smile and extended his hand to heartily shake mine as he usually did.

"Hello, stranger. How have you been? What have you been doing this summer?"

Without hesitation I blurted out the news about my acceptances to law school and that I got married. His eyes never left mine as he listened without saying a word. After I finished, he smiled politely, congratulated me on getting accepted to law school and getting married. And then, with an uncharacteristic coolness, he called out to one of his law clerks and asked about a matter he was working on. The law clerk approached with a file in hand. The judge congratulated me again and told me to take care as he turned away, entered his office, and closed the door.

A couple of weeks later, a few days before the first day of law school, I received a letter from the judge. He wrote:

Dear Kathy:
I trust that you will make Villanova your total priority in terms of steady, continuous application because I have really gone out on a limb for you....

If, at this point, you do not have the pattern of your life sufficiently together, it would be better to not accept this opportunity than to go if you cannot give it your total energy and attention.

Good luck!

I was alone in my apartment. I dropped and sat at the foot of the bed. I read the letter over and over again. My first thought was, *The judge doesn't believe that I can make it in law school now that I'm married.* My chest tightened and tears welled in my eyes. Now, for the first time, I felt doubt and disappointment. Thoughts consumed me. *Have I messed up everything? I've let everybody down. I'm so sorry. I didn't mean to.*

I cried until I fell asleep.

* * *

The end of August 1973, I arrived at Villanova University Law School at 7:25 a.m. My first class was scheduled for 9:00. I was early because Michael drove me to school. He wanted to show me how quickly I could get to school from Bucks County, a suburb of Philadelphia where we lived, if I took the expressway. I never drove on the expressway before. I insisted that we leave at 7:00 just in case there was an accident on the expressway. I didn't want to be late for my first day. There wasn't an accident, and at that time of the morning, there was hardly any traffic. When I got to school, there were only a couple of cars in the parking lot, probably the maintenance staff. Michael smirked and gave me that 'I told you so' look before he asked if I wanted to get some breakfast. I was too uptight to eat before we left home. He said, "I don't want to make you late. There's a Howard Johnson's restaurant at the end of the street. Even if there is a multi-car pileup, you could walk and still get back to class before nine o'clock."

"You're so funny. Let's get something to eat."

After breakfast, Michael dropped me off at 8:15 a.m. and went to work.

I walked into the building, carrying all of my thick, hardcover law books in an oversized tan leather duffel bag. I bought the largest bag I could find to carry my books. I intended to always carry all of my books, just in case I had some spare time and wanted to prepare for another class. That damn bag was so heavy, but I got used to the pain.

I headed for the lecture hall where my first class, Real Property, was scheduled. It was still early and I was surprised to see so many people in the hallway headed to the lecture hall. I called out to a student as he rushed past me to go in the room, "Why is everyone here so early? Class doesn't start until nine o'clock, right?"

He slowed down just a bit, looking back at me over his shoulder. "It's the first class. The seat you pick will be your seat for the rest of the year in all classes. Somebody will come around and record the seats we pick. Everybody's here early to get a good seat."

I nodded and wondered, How did he know that? Why didn't I know that? The answer to this and other inside tricks would become obvious. I didn't know because I didn't know anybody who ever went to Villanova University Law School. The students who intentionally got here early knew the game.

I quickened my step and went in the room. There were approximately 200 seats in the lecture hall, more than enough seats for the 105 students in section B of the first-year class. I took a seat on the third row, third seat from the end, under a large clock which hung on the wall. I sat between two white male students. Men outnumbered women in the first-year class by two to one, but this was a significant increase in the number of women. The guy who sat on my left smiled and nodded hello. The guy on my right was talking to another student and kept his back to me. When class started, he looked straight ahead. A few days later, after passing by each other before and after every class, we finally acknowledged each other with a nod.

The clerk who was to record our seats during the first class, for some unknown reason, didn't show up. I stayed in my seat. Since I had all of my books with me, I reviewed the material assigned for the next class, which was not until 11 a.m. I also listened as other students talked about the professors and what they expected first year to be like. Some students remained in the room; others left and took their books with them. That's when the trouble started.

Students moved into seats that other students sat in during the first class. When the students came back and saw someone in the seat that they had picked earlier, arguments erupted. I couldn't believe it. I never saw students argue over seats at Penn and certainly not in high school. What was this all about? You could see and hear no matter where you sat.

Before these future lawyers came to blows, the professor arrived. He told everyone to take the same seat they were in during the first class. The clerk from the Registrar's Office came and recorded the seats we were assigned for all classes for the year. A large seating chart was prepared with our names on it for the professors to use when calling on us in class. I learned later that some students were told by upperclassmen, friends, or relatives who went to Villanova University Law School about certain professors' habits when calling on students. That's why some students wanted or didn't want to sit on certain rows or in certain areas in the room.

By the end of that first day, I concluded that law school was seriously cutthroat and I'd better get ready.

* * *

Life as newlyweds wasn't going as either Michael or I anticipated. Since we had not planned to get married or that I would quit my job as a schoolteacher and go to law school at the end of the summer, we had some serious adjustments to make. Because of the study demands of law school, first-year students were urged strongly not to work, not even part-time. Since I didn't have a job, Michael worked three jobs, two full-time, one as an elementary school teacher during the day and a counselor at a school for special needs children overnight. He also worked part-time on Friday and all day Saturday at Leo's men's clothing store. Michael traded in his beautiful metallic-grey Mustang Mach I and bought a car that got better gas mileage, a drab-green Chevy Vega that gave him problems soon after he bought it. There was a national gas shortage, high prices and long lines at the gas stations. We both needed a car but could only afford one car note. I drove a 1965 Plymouth Barracuda that I bought with what was left in my student loan account after I graduated from college early.

Friends, many newlyweds like us, often called to invite us to go away for the weekend or just to hang out after work or on the weekends. Michael responded for us. "Hey, that sounds like fun, but we're going to have to pass this time. Kathy has got to study. Give us a call next time."

Our social life was limited to going out on Friday or Saturday night, rarely both. I don't think that's what Michael expected when we eloped.

In college I was glad that my boyfriend was away in the Army. I often joked that an away boyfriend was much better than a present one because I was free to go where I wanted, when I wanted, and with whom I wanted. I felt differently in law school. I was glad that in addition to all the challenges that law school presented, I didn't have to engage in the drama of being a woman playing the singles game in hopes of finding at least a steady relationship, even if it wasn't expected to be permanent. In law school and after, when I entered the dark caves which the legal profession represented for a young black woman in the mid-1970s, to have a supportive, loving husband around was a tremendous benefit.

When I was interviewed during the law school application process, Associate Dean Jackson asked if I was prepared to study 10 hours a day, every day. I answered yes. But I thought he must be kidding. I never had to study that much for anything. I thought that he was just trying to scare me. As a first-year law student, I studied at least 10 hours a day and more if I could. I arrived at school early and stayed late. I was totally consumed with the work required to prepare for class. I didn't think much about the load Michael carried and the sacrifices he had to make for me to pursue my dream. It all happened so fast. Michael and I jumped into marriage; it was only afterwards that we found out how deep we were in and what we had to do to make it through.

Whatever Dad said to Michael when he took him aside after we eloped didn't seem to frighten him, but it strengthened his resolve. Not only was no one ever going to say that I didn't become a lawyer because of Michael, they would never say he wasn't willing to do whatever was necessary to support me. That's the way he was reared by his parents, James and Gladys Lewis, and a large, strong, close-knit family.

As quickly as we got married, the course we were assigned to follow was rolled out before us. I was off to law school. Before we got married, Michael talked about going to graduate school. When I asked when he planned to take the graduate school exam and begin to take courses, he said he wasn't ready yet and it was my turn now. With only one of us working, the weight of supporting both of us was on Michael. He never complained as he worked three jobs. I avoided asking Michael for money and didn't want him to spend money unnecessarily. My fear of going into debt and Michael's desire for a comfortable home and time for fun when he wasn't working put us on a collision course.

On our first anniversary, I came home from school and found a beautiful multicolored area rug on the living room floor in our apartment; it was a great improvement over the worn carpet that was there when we moved in. There was also a new entertainment center in place of the prefab wooden shelves and painted cinder blocks Michael had before we got married, a new teak coffee table, and a large-screen television, which replaced the 13-inch screen that was there when I left for school that morning. There was a vase of flowers on the coffee table with an anniversary card from Michael. Everything was beautiful. My first thought was, we can't afford this. Where was Michael going to get the money for all of this stuff?

When he got home from his part-time job, he expected to find me surprised and overjoyed. Instead I was stressed and worried about how we were going to pay for everything. Michael's disappointment with my response ignited his temper. He shouted as he reminded me that he worked three jobs, paid all the bills, that he deserved a nice place to come home to, and he wasn't taking any of it back. I screamed that "we can't afford all of this stuff" as I went to the bedroom and slammed the door.

After a while Michael came into the bedroom, lay across the bed, and grabbed my hand. I tried to pull it away but he wouldn't let go. He said, "We both work hard and deserve some nice things. I know what I'm doing and how I'm going to pay for everything. Don't worry about it. It's our anniversary and I just wanted to surprise you. Come on, let's go out for dinner." I was strong-willed but so was he. We had to grow and find a way to compromise on how to handle finances.

Michael made sure that our life was about more than work and school. We slept in on Sunday mornings; in the afternoon I studied and he watched football before we went to one of our parents' houses for dinner. After dinner we came home and Michael fell asleep on the sofa in front of the television for a couple of hours before he went to his overnight job as a counselor at a residential facility for children.

Michael advanced on his job; he became a unit manager, a union representative, and ultimately a supervisor. Michael got along well with administrators, co-workers, and residents. It was not unusual for him to see a former resident on the street and stop to talk. If they spotted him first, they would call out, "Hey, Mr. Mike." When Michael committed to something, he was all in.

One morning I was on my way to school when I remembered that I forgot a book that I needed for class. I drove back home to get it. Michael left before me every day and picked up two co-workers on his way to work. When I arrived back at our apartment, I was surprised to see Michael's car there. I quickly got out of my car and ran onto the porch and unlocked the front door.

The first thing I noticed was that every light in the apartment was on. Anitra, one of the co-workers Michael drove to work with, was sitting on the sofa. Suddenly I was aware of a horrible smell. There was a commotion at the back of the apartment in the bathroom, and Michael came out of the bedroom calling out to Dan, the other co-worker he drove to work, "Here, let him put these jeans on. They belong to Kathy but they should fit him." I saw Dan in the bathroom with a towel in his hand, and someone else was in there with him.

I struggled to understand what the hell was going on. I said, loud enough to draw everyone's attention to the fact that I had come in, "Whoa! Michael, what's going on?"

Michael threw my pants to Dan and came toward me.

"Hey, we were on our way to work when I saw Jake at 52nd and Market Street. He's the boy I told you about who ran away from the Center a few days ago. I called him to come to me and he started to run. I had to chase him. He's been in the same clothes and gone to the bathroom on himself for days, I guess. I couldn't drive him in my car back to the Center like that. So, I brought him here to wash him up and get some clean clothes. I'll open the windows before we leave and I'll clean everything up when I come home."

Anitra nodded, affirming this unbelievable story. She said, "Michael chased Jake up the El steps, and that boy jumped over the turnstile and Michael jumped over it too. I was shouting oh, no! I was afraid a train was coming or the cops might lock both of them up."

I looked at Michael and just shook my head; I didn't know what to say. I grabbed my book, still shaking my head. I said, "I'll see you later." I went off to do what I needed to do and Michael did what he had to do.

Later, when I told my family about this incident, I said, "Let me tell you about my husband, the new member of the team of Starsky and Hutch." As I embellished the story with my knack for dramatic exaggeration, Michael's attempts to correct my tale usually ended with him saying, "I had to catch him and take him back to the Center. I couldn't leave him out there like that."

* * *

I didn't dare ask Mom or Dad for any help after I got married. They never told me that I couldn't come to them if I needed to. But I was the one who decided to run off and get married before I found out I was accepted to law school. I was told growing up, "If you make your bed hard, you have to lie in it." It was my responsibility to find a way to do what I needed to do and get what I needed to get.

After a few months it appeared that Michael and I were

handling things pretty well. Dad was not as tense as he was when we first got married. I sensed that he was optimistic that I was still going to become a lawyer. But after what I did, he kept his defenses up. He wasn't going to let me surprise or disappoint him again. I knew that some people thought that I was pregnant when I eloped or would soon get pregnant and quit school. I remembered what the men in the barbershop told Dad about it being a waste of money to send a girl to college. Dad used to say, "What people think doesn't determine what you can do. You do."

We usually went to one of our parents' houses for dinner on Sundays because my cooking skills were extremely limited, and that was a very generous assessment. Anything that took more than 30 minutes from concept to table to prepare was beyond my ability and interests. Every Sunday either my mom or Michael's mother insisted that we take some food home with us.

Not long into my first semester of law school, with all the reading required, I needed eyeglasses. I mentioned it one Sunday afternoon when we were at my parents' house for dinner. Dad called me the next day and asked when I could go to the eye doctor. He wanted to make an appointment for me with his doctor to have my eyes examined and buy my glasses.

I hesitated. "Dad, you don't have to do that. I'm going to get them." Dad had always told us that when we got married or moved out of the house, we were on our own. I didn't want him to think that I couldn't take care of myself. I already disappointed him enough. I wasn't looking for him to buy what I needed.

"I know Michael will buy glasses for you. Look, I am your daddy and if I can help you, I'm going to do that. Now, when can I take you to the eye doctor? You got a lot of reading to do. You need to get those glasses as soon as possible," Dad said.

Even after I disappointed him, Dad still loved me and was

in my corner, pulling for me to succeed. It felt good to know that my family still believed in me. But I learned that I was the only one empowered to abandon my dream.

* * *

All first-year students were required to take Moot Court, which included writing a memorandum of law and a legal brief, and presenting an oral argument. There were two students assigned to a team; one team represented the plaintiff and another team represented the defendant in a mock trial. A professor was assigned to supervise and grade approximately eight teams. Jeff, an African American student, and I decided to work as a team. I didn't know Jeff before law school, but his sister and I went to Penn together. Professor Rosen was assigned to supervise the group of students that included our team. Upperclassmen, blacks and whites, warned students assigned to Professor Rosen that he was tough on first-year students. They called him "Killer Rosen." Professor Rosen required all students to read the case file and prepare a statement of the issues. He evaluated the issues submitted by each team, and if he approved, the team could begin to research and write their memorandum of law.

Jeff and I submitted a statement of issues to him three times. After the third time, Professor Rosen said, "I am still not satisfied with your statement of issues, but you are already at least two weeks behind everyone else. You might as well go ahead and get started, but you still need to work on the issues." Jeff and I knew that Professor Rosen had already given the go-ahead to the other students, but at least now we could get started.

We completed the research and submitted our memorandum of law, with a revised statement of issues, on time. A conference was scheduled to critique our memorandum and our opponents'. Professor Rosen and two students from the Moot Court Board read the memoranda and were at the conference, along with our opponents. Our opponents were two white male students and we were all about the same age. They were in the other section of the first-year class. They were friendly and clearly as anxious as we were to get through this conference. Moot Court, like everything else about first year, was learning through fear and intimidation. I learned quickly no matter what happened, never let anyone see you sweat. Preparation and determination were the best defenses.

All day before the conference, my stomach was in knots. At least the conference was scheduled on a Friday at the end of the day, which meant I would have a couple of days to shake off the beating I expected from Killer Rosen. What I dreaded most was that he was going to shoot us down in front of other people. At least when Professor Rosen told us our statement of issues was not acceptable, it was just Jeff and me in his office. I thought, Oh, what the hell, let's just get it over with.

The conference room was on the second floor, across from the registrar's office. It was a very formal room with a long, dark-red mahogany conference table surrounded by high-back, tufted, burgundy leather chairs. There was a large window covered with thick, cream-colored draperies. I knew it was still daylight outside, but with the drapes closed, there was no light from the outside. It was late fall, cool enough to wear a light jacket. The conference room was cold, as if the air conditioner had been on all day. I tried to amuse myself. I thought, Isn't hell supposed to be hot? So why is it cold in here? Now that I was in the room, I braced myself. My heart beat quickly and I willed it to slow down, folded my hands, and kept my eyes on our memorandum. Jeff and I worked our butts off, researching, writing, editing up until the day we turned it in. I didn't care what Rosen said. I intended to listen, keep my mouth shut, and get out of there. That's it!

The conference began with Professor Rosen stating that he was going to review our opponents' memorandum first. He proceeded to go page by page, line by line, picking out every error, legal form, sentence structure, punctuation, citations, deficient legal analysis, etc. The room was funeral quiet. The only voice was Professor Rosen's. Once or twice he pressed one of our opponents to answer a question. By now the palms of my hands began to sweat. I sat still and kept my eyes on our memorandum. I felt my opponents' discomfort. I held on for what Professor Rosen was going to do to us.

After he finished our opponents off, he turned to Jeff and me. "Based on the difficulty that the two of you had in getting the issues properly framed, I didn't expect you to do well researching and writing a memorandum of law. But I must say I was surprised. This is one of the best memoranda of law I have ever received from first-year students. There were still some minor matters that I'll go over with you when I get back." Then he left the room.

I felt a smile coming to my face. I wanted to jump up from the table, spin around, and give Jeff a high five. But the smile never appeared and I remained still.

Professor Rosen returned in about five minutes and went over our memorandum. When he finished, he looked coldly at our opponents and said, "Before I came here this afternoon, I reviewed all of your undergraduate records, which are on file in the registrar's office."

For emphasis, he pointed around the table at all of us before he redirected his attention to our opponents and continued.

"Now I know if they can do it..." This time, without looking in our direction, he pointed to Jeff and me. "...I know you can do it. I expect your brief to be very much improved next semester."

With that, the conference ended.

I know my face contorted. What he said kept bouncing off the walls of my head. It felt like I had been backhand-slapped across the face.

Jeff and I walked down the steps and stood quietly in the hall for a few minutes. I repeated Professor Rosen's words.

"'If they can do it, I know you can do it'? What is that supposed to mean?"

Jeff shook his head and said, "I'm sure he didn't want to admit that it was one of the best memoranda he ever received from first-year students. Let's get out of here. I'm glad it's over."

I learned that my ability was not determined by people who had low, or worse, no expectations that I could succeed.

So, what was next?

13

Handling the Retest

Perhaps it would have been easy to deal with all the first-year law school stuff if it only came from professors.

As a first-year law student, I didn't know the ropes—the unwritten rules, strategic maneuvers, reputations or idiosyncrasies of the professors. Many second- and third-year students shared information intended to help first-year students navigate the waters or at least keep from drowning. Some just shared war stories to keep us on edge.

At the end of the first semester, there was a reading period before exams started. From day one, second- and third-year students warned us, "Stay up on your assignments, do the reading, start outlining the material now. Don't wait until the end of the semester to get ready for exams." I listened and followed their advice.

Everyone knew that students selected study groups after the first few weeks of school. At first I assumed that these groups came about as the result of informal networking or new friendships. I watched how students aligned into study groups and saw that it was more than just that. Students wanted to study with people they thought were at least as smart as they were, willing to work, and who would make a contribution to the study group. But it was not an open selection process. One black student tried to join a study group of six white students. They gave her the runaround. The meeting locations or times were changed and no one told her. Repeatedly, she was given lame excuses to explain the "mix-ups." It was obvious they didn't want her in their group. After a few weeks she got the message and stopped trying to join them. I wasn't surprised. I learned the first day of class that law school was cutthroat. Library books that students needed to prepare for exams went missing. It was not unusual to find pages torn out of books required to complete research assignments. This caused big problems as students desperately tried to complete assignments on time or prepare for exams. Sometimes I went to the law library at other schools in the city to study.

The black second-year students urged black first-year students to form a study group. They knew that it wasn't likely that we would be invited or welcomed to join any of the white groups. There were eight black students in my class, and two of them were repeating first year. I never studied in a group before. In college sometimes I studied with other people but that only meant that they were in the same room. Everyone did their own thing with little or no input from anyone else. I decided to follow the crowd and take the advice of those who had made it through first year.

The exam period approached. I reviewed the notes and outlines I prepared during the year. I was ready for the first group study session. It was the second day of the reading period, a time allotted for students to prepare to take exams. Hope and dread were my constant companions. Tension stretched every nerve in my body to the limit. Just stay focused.

Seven of us met at the law school in a small locker room with a long wooden table surrounded by metal folding chairs. The only person missing was Jason. None of us knew where he was or why he wasn't there. We expected him to study with us. We couldn't wait or go look for him. We plunged into the material that we needed to review for our first exam, which was Real Property, one of the more difficult courses. The plan was to briefly discuss the facts, reasoning, and holding of the cases that were covered during the semester, state the legal principles, and move on. I thought this would be simple. I was wrong.

This group study session was a total disaster. Some students were well prepared with a good grasp of the material. A few were not and they wanted to debate every point with those who were. After a couple of hours, before we broke for lunch, I knew this group process wasn't going to work for me. But I stayed until the session ended late that afternoon. We studied together for almost seven-and-a-half hours and didn't cover half of the material we planned to review. The exam was scheduled for the day after next.

Jeff and I walked to the parking lot together. I was totally wiped out, frustrated and more anxious than ever about the upcoming exam. I learned in high school and college that if following the crowd caused problems for me, I had to change course. I told Jeff, "I am not coming back to the study group tomorrow. I can't do this."

With an exasperated chuckle he said, "I was thinking the same thing."

We walked in silence until we reached my car, and then Jeff said, "Why don't we study by ourselves in the morning and meet at your place or mine for a couple of hours in the afternoon to go over the material. After we meet, we can go back and continue to study on our own."

I liked the idea of having someone to bounce ideas off of, but I didn't want to get bogged down in a big study group. This study plan made more sense and so Jeff and I followed it. After the second exam, Edward, another black student, noticed that Jeff and I stopped coming to the large study group. He asked if we were studying together and could he join us. We told him how our informal study sessions worked and he was welcome to study with us. Jason, the student who didn't show up the first day of the large study group session, dropped out of law school before the first exam. Now there were seven black first-year students.

One afternoon before the first-semester grades came out, a few second-year students and about five first-year students were in the Black Law Students Office. This was a small room where black students frequently gathered throughout the day to regroup, commiserate, or blow off steam. Most student organizations had offices in the law school. There were approximately 16 black students in the entire school. At that time there were not any black full-time professors. There was only one white woman on the faculty. She was the librarian and taught legal research. Black students needed a place to breathe and to share experiences, thoughts, and feelings that were different from the nearly 600 white students, professors, and administrators at the law school.

On that afternoon Clark, a second-year student, said to the first-year students in the room, "I heard that some of you didn't participate in the group study sessions. I hope you know what you're doing. We've been through this stuff. Let me tell you, the study group is really important."

I knew his comments were directed at me and Jeff because we were the first to break rank and stop coming to the study group. Now we were being called out for not following their advice. It was as if a steam valve on a pipe that had exceeded its threshold for containment broke open inside of me. I froze. I thought about the lessons Dad taught me: "Don't ride the red horse. Control your emotions, don't let your emotions control you." He also taught me, "Don't follow the crowd. Think for yourself." And to do what I believed to be right. As I remembered these "Streeterisms," I kept my mouth shut, and the valve that contained my temper slowly closed.

With a calm that even surprised me, I looked directly into Clark's eyes and said, "I never studied in groups before. That just doesn't work for me."

I took a deep breath. At that moment I was proud of myself. My tone was direct but not apologetic. I hoped I sent a clear message that let Clark know—don't take me to a place you don't want me to go. Quiet blanketed the room; all eyes were on me. I sensed that Clark and everyone else in the room knew how I felt.

Bridgett, also a second-year student, jumped up from her seat at the other end of the table. She raised her voice, pointed her finger at me, and said, "You better listen! Who do you think you are? You're not going to make it if—"

Before she finished, I jumped up from my seat, raised my voice even louder, and said, "I am going to do what works for me. You do what works for you. If what I do causes me to fail, it will be on my terms and I'll deal with it. But I'll be damned if I fail for doing what you tell me to do. Your way doesn't work for me!"

We were both on our feet, glaring at each other. Everyone in the room sat up straight, remained still, and didn't say a word. Clark went toward Bridgett and held his arms out as if to hold her back.

"Don't hold her back," I yelled.

Now a few of the other students quickly got to their feet. "Wait a minute, wait a minute," they shouted.

It was obvious where this was headed. I grabbed my overstuffed duffel bag and left the room.

Later that afternoon I was on my way to class when Jeff caught up to me. He laughed and said, "Hey, I didn't know you carried boxing gloves in that big bag." Still laughing, he slapped me on the shoulder and said, "One thing for sure: you don't have to worry about anyone inviting you to any group study sessions after today."

It was a cold day in the middle of January 1974 when I received my first-semester grades. I passed all my classes with a grade-point average that placed me in the top third of the class. First, I called Michael and told him the news. Next, I called Judge Higginbotham's chambers and scheduled an appointment to meet with him later that week. When I showed him my grades, he smiled and said, "Keep up the good work." When I showed my grades to Dad, he said, "That's good, I knew you could do it."

I breathed a sigh of relief. I was still on track. By the time first year ended, I understood what was required for me to own my dream.

14

Prepare to Go to Work

The summer after first-year law school, I worked as an intern in the Regional Counsel's Office of the Department of Housing and Urban Development (HUD). Judge Higginbotham recommended me for the internship after I told him I had applied. The Regional Counsel was William F. Hall, Esquire, a serious, intelligent, concerned man. He and the judge had been attorneys in a very highly respected black law firm in Philadelphia (Norris, Green, Harris, Schmidt and Higginbotham) before their current positions.

Mr. Hall was very interested in helping interns learn the ins and outs of the practice of law. He let me sit in on meetings with department heads, outside counsel, and staff meetings. Once I sat in on a meeting he had with a community group from the Society Hill section of the city. They came in to protest funding decisions by the federal government that blocked the development of housing for low-income families in gentrifying neighborhoods in Philadelphia. After the meeting, Mr. Hall asked me to draft a memorandum concerning the issues raised by the community group. Based on my research, I believed that HUD's funding policies reinforced the status quo. And as a result, poor and minority residents were relegated to declining neighborhoods with substandard housing. They were forced out when upper-income people moved into the area and built houses that the current residents couldn't afford. The only way people who had lived in the community, in some cases for generations, could afford to stay in the area was if HUD provided funding for the development of housing for low- and moderate-income families. Mr. Hall was impressed with my analysis.

The summer was going well. Stanley Belcher, a senior attorney in the office, wanted me to go to another office and pick up a file for a case he was working on. I sat in a small cubicle outside of his office. His door was open and I heard him talking on the telephone. Mr. Belcher was an old white man who talked very loud. I thought he was a little hard of hearing. He said to the person he was talking to, "I want to see your file, I'm going to send our girl over to get it. I'll tell her to ask for you. She will let you know that she's the girl from HUD. I'll call you back after I review the file."

He hung up and yelled out to me, "Hey, are you there?"

I didn't answer. I seethed, Did he just call me "girl," "our girl"?

Mr. Belcher called out again, "Hey, are you there?"

I still didn't answer. He came to the door of his office and looked around it and into my cubicle. He told me to go and pick up a file from the program office downstairs. He said, "I just got off the phone with Jack. Tell him you're the girl from HUD and I sent you to get the file."

Slowly I pushed my chair back from my grey metal desk and turned to face him. "I am not anybody's girl. Let me ask you this—is the girl from HUD like the Man from U.N.C.L.E.?"

Mr. Belcher looked confused and brusquely said, "What? I don't know. Just get that file and bring it to me." He shook his head and went back into his office.

I said loud enough for him and anyone else close by to hear, "I am not your girl. Just understand that."

Pissed off, I marched to the program office, retrieved the file, and went to Mr. Belcher's office. I tried to make eye contact with him as I handed him the file. I wanted him to see that I was angry. He never looked up.

"Just put it down," he said.

I placed the file on his desk and went back to my cubicle. I'd never disrespected Mr. Belcher or anyone else in the office. He treated me like I was nothing. He acted as if I didn't have a right to tell him not to call me "girl."

I went to Mr. Hall's office and told him what happened and what I said to Mr. Belcher. I didn't know if Mr. Belcher was going to say anything to him. But if I was going to lose my internship or get a bad evaluation for what I said to him, I wanted Mr. Hall to hear my side.

He sat back in his chair; his eyes never left my face as he listened to what I had to say. He never smiled and his serious expression never changed. After I finished, I saw his jaw tighten. He nodded his head slowly. "I'll look into this. No one should refer to you or any of the women in this office as 'girl.'"

Later that afternoon, Mr. Hall called an unexpected staff meeting. Everyone in the office, including attorneys, clerical staff, and interns, came into the conference room. The attorneys and a few of the interns sat around the long conference table; the clerical staff and paralegals sat along the walls. The room did not have any windows. The glare from the overhead fluorescent lights brightly lit the room. People whispered, "What's going on?"

Mr. Hall sat at the head of the table and waited for everyone to come into the room and take a seat. With a clenched jaw, eyes dark and penetrating, he looked around the room before he said anything. "I have something important to talk to you about."

Then he told them what happened between me and Mr. Belcher. Everyone kept their eyes on Mr. Hall. He spent the next few minutes talking about respect. The last things he said before the meeting ended was, "Everybody has the right to be treated with respect. Everyone in this office will treat everyone who works here or comes to this office for any reason with respect. If anyone here thinks that you cannot do that, you should find someplace else to work."

His expression never changed. And his controlled, stern tone of voice left no mistake that he meant what he said. It reminded me of when I was 13 and Dad gave Buck, the first boy who came to see me, a lesson in respect.

Mr. Belcher didn't say anything else to me for the rest of the summer. A couple of the female clerical staff told me they were glad I spoke up. One secretary said, "Mr. Belcher always treats women, except the only woman attorney in the office, like children."

A few days after the meeting, Maria, a young, white secretary who was about my age, said, "You people take everything so personal. Mr. Belcher didn't mean nothin' by what he said to you. He's just old. To him you are a little girl."

She stood back from me, shifted from one foot to the other, and her voice cracked. I could tell she had to get her nerve up to say that to me. She didn't want a confrontation but she felt the need to defend Mr. Belcher. She didn't understand that I was sick and tired of grown black women being called "girl." I knew many black women who did "days-work," cared for white children, or worked as live-in housekeepers and only saw their own families on weekends. They were referred to by the people they worked for as "our girl." It was 1974. Everyone knew that it was offensive to call a black man "boy." Well, it was time to stop calling fully grown, working black women "girls."

I didn't explain my history or my feelings to Maria. Perhaps I should have. I said, "Like I told him and now I'm telling you, I'm not a girl. Don't call me that."

My internship was a peek into what lay ahead in the world of work. I learned a lot about the practice of law and attitudes of some people in the workplace. I didn't intend to make enemies or to make anyone uncomfortable. But if the price to be tolerated, though not accepted, meant keeping quiet when others disrespected me—I was not willing to pay it.

15

Knocked Off My Square

The second year of law school got off to a good start. It was not as intense as first year. There were still some difficult courses and even more difficult professors, but the fear was gone.

A few days into the second semester, on January 9, 1975, without warning an earthquake shook my world. My baby sister Marilyn, who we called Reese, was stabbed and left to die inside a car on a vacant used car lot in Chestnut Hill, an upscale section of Philadelphia. She was 13 years old.

The newspaper headlines read:

Sitter Stabbed 25 Times
(*Philadelphia Daily News*, Thursday, January 9, 1975)

Stabbed Sitter's Kin In Hospital Vigil
(*The Evening Bulletin*, Thursday, January 9, 1975)

> The family of Marilyn Streeter kept a lonely vigil at Chestnut Hill Hospital last night. 'We intend to stay here until we know she's getting better,' said John Streeter, 50, Marilyn's father. 'This was brutal, vicious, savage and animalistic ...naturally I feel bad and mad.'

(*The Evening Bulletin*, Thursday, January 9, 1975)

Early in the morning on January 9, 1975, Reese was found stumbling across a vacant car lot located in Chestnut Hill, Philadelphia. The night before, she was on her way home from babysitting for a former neighbor who had recently moved from North Philadelphia, where my parents lived. Rob, the father of the children Reese was babysitting, was driving her home. His body was found lying in the street hours before Reese was discovered a few blocks away. He had been shot and killed. When Reese was found stumbling across that vacant car lot, the ice pick used to stab her repeatedly protruded from her back.

Early that evening, Michael and I went out to dinner to celebrate his birthday. The weather forecast was unusually warm for early January. But unexpectedly, it turned very cold. When we got home that night, about 11:00, my friend Pauline called. "Hey, Kathy, how's Reese doing?"

I was caught off-guard and confused. Why was she calling at this time of night to ask me that? "Fine, why do you ask?"

An awkward silence before she said, "Kathy, you don't know?"

I could tell by the tone of her voice that she was sorry she'd called.

"It's been all over the news. Reese was found stabbed this morning in Chestnut Hill. Nobody told you?"

"What? I gotta go!"

I hung up and called my parents. Dad answered the phone.

"What happened to Reese?"

"She's in the hospital and we just got home. How did you find out? I was going to call you, but I needed to talk to the doctors first. How did you find out?"

"Pauline just called. She said it's been on the news. What happened to her?"

"She was babysitting for Sandra. The best we know right now is that Rob was driving her home. Rob's car was found on a vacant car lot, and the police believe that's where Reese was stabbed and left in the car. I guess whoever did this thought she was dead too. Somehow she got out of the car and was found stumbling around Chestnut Hill this morning."

I covered my mouth. My heart pounded so hard my chest hurt. "Oh my God. No, no!"

I dropped into the chair next to the desk and gripped the telephone, crying and shaking. I asked, "Dad, is she going to make it?"

He paused for a long time, and a chill went through me. Dad tried to be strong, sound confident, but he couldn't hide that he just didn't know. "I think she's gonna make it. The doctors said the puncture wounds just missed most of her major organs. Her lungs were punctured and she was in surgery all day. She was resting when me and your mother left the hospital a little while ago. Don't worry, I think she's gonna be okay. You want to talk to your mother?" Quickly he handed the phone to Mom.

Still sobbing, I wanted to know more. I repeated everything Dad said so Michael, who paced nearby, could hear. Michael whispered to me, "Do you want to go over there or to the hospital?"

Mom got on the phone. She was trying not to cry but heart-wrenching sadness was in every word. From the depths of her pain sprung an unalterable proclamation of faith that she clung to. It helped her keep it together as she told me what happened.

"I felt something was not right yesterday when Reese wasn't home by nine o'clock. She's usually always home by that time. Last week, I told Sandra that Reese could only babysit for a couple weeks. She was going to have to find someone else to watch her kids now that she moved from around here. Reese wasn't going to be coming home late every night. I definitely knew something was wrong when she wasn't here by ten o'clock. But my mind told me my baby was alive. God is going to bring her through this, I know He will."

In disbelief Mom described how Reese looked when she and Dad left the hospital and tried to imagine how this happened. "She just looked so pitiful lying in that bed. I know she was scared. How could anybody do that to a little girl? She must've been fighting for all she was worth. That's why they couldn't do what they really wanted. And the doctors said that because she had on so many layers of clothes, and the unexpected drop in the temperature worked in her favor. The cold stopped the bleeding at the location of the most serious wounds."

Now I was crying so hard I couldn't talk. Michael grabbed the telephone from me and told Mom that we were going to the hospital.

Dad got back on the phone. "Mike, please don't take Kathy to the hospital tonight. Wait until tomorrow. If we hear anything, I'll call you right away. Take care of Kathy. All we can do now is wait."

The next day at the hospital, my younger sister Ellen filled me and Michael in about what happened before Mom and Dad found out that Reese had been stabbed. Ellen told us that when Reese wasn't home by midnight, Mom called Dad at work and he came home. He called Sandra, then he began calling the hospitals. When there was no information about Reese or Rob, Dad called the police. About 1:00 in the morning, Sandra called and said that Rob's body was found. Mom asked her, "What about Reese? Where is she?"
Ellen heard Sandra crying on the phone when she told Mom the police didn't know anything about Reese. They were looking for Rob's car.

Dad called the police and told them, "My thirteen-year-old daughter was in that car with the man you found dead on Germantown Avenue. Have you found her?"

The police told Dad that they were looking for the car and would call him as soon as they knew anything. At 6:00 in the morning, police detectives knocked on the door and said, "Mr. Streeter, we found your daughter. She's been taken to Chestnut Hill Hospital. We'll take you there now."

Dad asked the police, "Is she alive?"

The detectives didn't answer. By the time Mom and Dad got to the hospital, Reese had been taken into surgery.

Later, Mom told me that the next morning before they went to the hospital, she went back upstairs and saw Dad sitting on the side of the bed, crying. "He just kept saying, 'I couldn't protect my baby from this. I should never have let her go up there to babysit after Sandra moved. God, don't let my baby die.'"

Mom said that she hugged him and said, "God is going to take care of her. I know it."

In a daze, I tried to go about my usual routine. I wondered how was I expected to keep myself together when life crashed down on my family like this. I went to school every day, tried to pay attention, read the assignments, and took notes. I retained nothing. I didn't tell Michael, Dad, or anyone that I planned to take a leave of absence. I wanted to be at the hospital with Reese.

As if he knew what I was thinking, Dad insisted that I go to school. He told me that there wasn't anything any of us could do at the hospital. I didn't want to upset him even more by telling him my plan. I obeyed and kept going to school. Every day as soon as classes ended, instead of staying at school to study as usual, I drove to the hospital and sat by Reese's bed.

Dad talked to the police daily to inquire about possible suspects. He and my brother, Johnny, canvassed the neighborhood to get the word on the street and find out if anyone knew who did this to Reese. The police were concerned that once Reese's attackers found out she was alive, they would come for her. One afternoon I heard Dad talking with the detectives about the progress of the investigation. He asked did they have any suspects. Then he said, "I swear to God, I'll kill 'em if I find them before the police. Your search will be over and you can just come here and lock my butt up. I won't run."

Dad could not protect us from everything but nothing could stop him from trying. I watched his anger give way to gratitude to God for sparing Reese's life. The hospital bills for Reese's extended stays and repeated surgeries cost more than Dad's insurance covered. He went to the finance office of Chestnut Hill Hospital and agreed to pay whatever was owed.

"That hospital, the doctors and nurses there saved my baby's life. I'm going to do my best to pay 'em."

After Reese came home from the hospital, I settled down. I eased back into what had been my study routine and stayed at school later before I went to visit Reese every day. It was important to me that she knew that I was there for her. Mom urged me to go home and get some rest. That was always Mom's admonition to me: "Kathy, get some rest, slow down, for goodness sakes."

"Reese is alright," Dad said. "Nothing is going to happen to her. You need to get back in your books. You can call. Come by on the weekends."

* * *

Back at school unnerving tension plummeted to a new low. Someone scrawled on the desk in the Black Law Students Office *Fuck you niggers you'll never be a good law student*. Black students were angry and complained to the dean. But on a positive note, the law school hired a female professor, Mary Jo Frug, to teach courses related to race and sex discrimination. I couldn't wait to take her classes. Student Faculty Committee elections were scheduled and several black students urged me to run for a committee. I was reluctant for a lot of reasons. One, I didn't have time and I thought that this was just an exercise, posturing. It wasn't that my militant marching, outspoken days were over. But the only march I wanted to focus on now was the one that led to graduation from this place. Even though I was not enthusiastic, I agreed to run for the Grading and Exam Committee. I was elected.

Just when it seemed as if things were getting back to normal, Reese had to go back in the hospital for another surgery. I tried to stay focused. I prayed that the world would right itself and stop spinning out of control. My emotions were on a roller-coaster. I didn't have any emotional capital or energy to spend on anything that did not have the ability to protect and sustain my family. The people I cared about centered me. I never wanted to forget that family mattered most.

As a family, we held each other's dreams, hopes, and lives so close to our hearts that a piece of us dwelled within every one of us. As I carried my sister's pain within me, so, too, she held my dream to become a lawyer. We carried each other. Our futures and our brighter days were inextricably linked.

16

Are We There Yet?

Now the finish line was in sight, or so I thought. The summer before my third year of law school, I worked as an intern for the U.S. Department of Health, Education, and Welfare and expected to work 15 hours per week during the school year. It was not a lot of money, but I sure could use it. I didn't want to ask Michael for money, even though he always offered. Instead I used money from my student loans or part-time jobs for anything I wanted. Michael paid for everything we needed. The least I could do was take care of my personal needs and school expenses. The Bar Examination was the big gorilla that I had to get around after law school, and I would need money for a bar review course, but I'd cross that bridge when I got to it. As I entered my final year of law school, all I wanted was some smooth sailing.

At the beginning of the school year, I was told to go to the associate dean's office. There were rumors floating around that the school intended to change the financial aid packages awarded to students in the past. But I wasn't worried. One thing was certain: even with my summer job, a part-time internship, and Michael's three jobs, my financial need had not changed. I could not pay the tuition required to attend law school.

When I arrived, Mr. Jackson, the associate dean, said,

"Hello, Mrs. Lewis, please come in. Have a seat. I am sure you're looking forward to your final year. This time next year you'll be one of our alumni."

I smiled and cautiously said, "I sure hope so."

He continued smiling as he tried to calm the waters for the message he was about to deliver. And my expression probably conveyed what I was thinking: Please cut the small talk, you didn't call me here to give me an early congratulations on completing law school. Let's get to it.

"I know that when you were accepted here for law school, you received a grant for the full tuition, and you received that same grant for your second year. But the school has decided that it is important that students who receive grants have a moral obligation to repay the law school. So this year you will receive financial aid in the full amount of the tuition, but it will be a loan, not a grant."

"What, a loan? Why? My financial position has not improved since I was admitted." I wasn't about to agree to this. When I was accepted to law school, I was promised a full ride, which included tuition and room and board. After I got married, I didn't accept the offer of room and board because it required me to live on campus and work as a counselor in the undergraduate girls' dormitory.

"We are aware of that. But it appears that you didn't borrow very much to pay for your undergraduate education at the University of Pennsylvania. So, you're in a position to apply for a loan from a private financial institution. If you don't want a loan from the law school, you could borrow the money from a bank. I know this comes as a surprise and regret having to do this…"

Dean Jackson just kept talking. Blah, blah, blah. I tuned him out. The long and the short of it was this: Take the loan we are offering, or try, at this late date, to borrow the money from a bank, or drop out in my last year of law school and come back when I could afford to pay.

I accepted the loan and told him that I didn't have much of

a choice. I stood up to leave but before I turned toward the door, Mr. Jackson slid a promissory note across his desk with my name on it. I looked down at it quickly and then at Mr. Jackson. "I thought this loan was supposed to be a moral obligation. Why do I have to sign this?" I said. I knew enough from first-year contracts that signing a promissory note was more than a moral obligation. This was a legal obligation.

"All students who receive tuition loans are required to sign a promissory note," Mr. Jackson said.

Our eyes locked. I nodded slowly and took a pen from my duffel bag. I ignored the pen he handed to me and signed the papers. I didn't want anything this man had to offer. Before I closed the door to his office, I turned to him and stated a fact I wanted him to think about. "I learned an important legal concept my first year of law school: 'Last in time, last in right.'"

That evening, I called Dad and told him what happened.

"Don't worry about it. They must think you going to be able to pay it or they wouldn't loan it to you. If the education you got at that school doesn't get you a job to pay back that loan, then you and that school will be out. Don't worry, do what you have to do to graduate," he said.

* * *

When the search for jobs began, things really got tense. Growing up, tough guys in the neighborhood, before going to fight, would say to the guys who didn't have the heart to fight, "If you can't run with the big dogs, you better stay on the porch." Then the tough guys would make a loud barking sound. To land a job was the payoff for all the years of school, anxiety, and expense. The process was very competitive. The fight was on.

It was 1975 and the job market was tight for newly minted, just-out-of-school lawyers. Villanova's on-campus interview process permitted prospective employers to screen resumes in advance before selecting from the list of students who applied for interviews. After reviewing the resumes, the employer would send a list of the students they selected to interview. Everyone not selected understood that the employer was not interested in considering them for a position. It was known that the large law firms, which paid the highest salaries, usually only interviewed students on law review or in the top 10 percent of the class. A few students who didn't meet those criteria signed up anyway and sometimes were selected for an interview.

I was surprised when one of the large law firms granted me an interview. I wasn't in the top 10 percent of the class, but I signed up for an interview anyway. I remembered my high school counselor telling me to never write myself off. If they failed to pick me, it would be their loss.

On the day of my interview, I wore one of my two interview suits—one grey, the other navy blue. I wore a white collared blouse with a burgundy necktie scarf. I dressed just like it was written in the book *Dress for Success*, which was code for dress like a man. I also got rid of my afro and straightened my hair. I pulled out all the stops to make a good impression.

I had complained to Dad, "Why do black people always have to assimilate to get ahead?"

"Look, it's not what's on your head; it's what's in it. You know who you are and what you stand for. All you want now is to get a job. Nobody can change what you think unless you let 'em. It don't matter how you wear your hair."

"Yeah, I hear you, but you know what I mean. It's not right."

When my name was called, I went into the room. Both of the interviewers, white male lawyers from the law firm, stood up to greet me. They smiled nervously, shook my hand, and motioned for me to sit down. Only one of the attorneys asked me any questions. He asked about some of the courses on my transcript and my majors at the University of Pennsylvania.

The other lawyer rarely looked up from the pile of folders that contained information about the other students who were on the list to be interviewed. It was obvious he considered my interview a waste of time. Most interviews lasted the full 20 minutes allotted. I know because I arrived early for the interview and waited outside as other students went in for their interviews. I arrived early because I wanted to hear what students said after the interview to their friends who may have been waiting, or I wanted to see the expression on their faces after the interview ended. My interview was over in 12 minutes. I timed it.

Community Legal Services (CLS), an organization that represented poor and minority residents in Philadelphia, also conducted on-campus interviews. Five of the seven black students signed up for an interview. At last, an employer that we expected to at least grant us an interview. We didn't know how many new attorneys CLS planned to hire, but our chances of getting a job offer were astronomically better than with any of the law firms or most of the government agencies. At least that's what we thought. When the list of the students selected for interviews was posted, none of the black students were on it. Four of us immediately asked to meet with the dean, who arranged for us to meet with an associate dean. We told him what happened and demanded that someone ask why CLS refused to interview any black students. We grumbled among ourselves when the other employers refused to interview us, but we never asked why because we knew the answer. Most of the employers had few, if any, black attorneys in their offices, and they were not planning to change the status quo. But CLS represented clients from the neighborhoods where we grew up, and we expected an opportunity to be considered for a position.

Sandy, a very outspoken black woman in our class, was furious. "This shit doesn't make any sense. The white firms and most of the government agencies won't even interview us. I guess we're not expected to have jobs after graduation.

This shit can't continue; we have to do something," she said.

Denise, another black woman in our class, bit her bottom lip and nodded. "I bet if we go to the media and the NAACP, somebody will listen. We all work too damn hard to let them shut us down like this," Denise said.

After our next class we agreed to go back to the dean to see if the administration was going to do anything about this. The associate dean told us that he called the hiring attorney at CLS and was told that he gave the list of students who requested interviews to Professor Washington to review and make recommendations. Professor Washington had worked at CLS before he came to the law school. Obviously he had not recommended any of us. Sandy, Denise, and I stormed off to see Professor Washington to ask him why he didn't recommend us. I was spitting mad as I thought about what I intended to say to Professor Washington. What is this? I took both of the classes that he taught, participated in class, and got good grades in both classes. Why didn't he recommend me for an interview? Sandy and Denise had taken one of his classes and also did well.

When we showed up, unannounced, uninvited, and clearly pissed off, Professor Washington was surprised. We confronted him with what we learned about his role in the process and asked why we were not selected to be interviewed by CLS. He invited us to have a seat in his small office and nervously said, "Oh, the hiring attorney sent me the list of students a few days ago, and I planned to go to the registrar's office to look at the students' pictures in the file. I'm better at remembering faces than I am with names. Frankly, I forgot to do that and when he called me to ask for my recommendations, it was early in the morning." He smiled nervously. We weren't smiling as we waited for an answer. He continued, "I had just gotten out of the shower. I still had shaving cream on my face. He read the names to me and as best I could, still half asleep, I said yes to the names I thought I recognized. I intended to check the photos on file to see if I knew any of the other names he mentioned. I admit that I forgot to do it, but it's not too late. I'll do it today and call him back."

Sandra rolled her eyes and Denise took a deep breath and looked up at the ceiling and just shook her head. I said, "I don't feel any better now that I know how you were going to decide who to recommend. My picture is not on file in the registrar's office because I never sent one in. In college the freshman photos were kept in a book on file and everyone called it the 'pig book.' So, I never sent a picture to the registrar. I guess without that picture, you would not have recommended me. I took both your classes, sat up front, you called on me regularly, and I earned a good grade. But you didn't recognize my name?"

He became defensive and his tone reflected that he was annoyed with being confronted. "As I said, it was early. I still had shaving cream on my face. Ms. Perry, I'm sure that when I looked at the list and compared it to my old class lists, I would have remembered and certainly would have recommended that you be granted an interview."

As soon as Professor Washington called me Ms. Perry, Denise and Sandy looked at me and fell back in their seats.

"Is that right? Professor Washington, my last name is Lewis, not Perry. Do you remember me now?" I asked.

At least now I understood that it was not the shave cream that caused him not to remember my name, even when he looked at my face. Without another word, we all got up and left his office. Later that afternoon a revised interview list for CLS was posted. Four of the five black students who signed up to be interviewed were added to the list. Three of us were offered positions as staff attorneys upon graduation.

* * *

In addition to on-campus interviews, I applied for several judicial clerkships. Judge Higginbotham suggested that I apply for a clerkship with his former law partner, Judge Doris May Harris, who was on the Pennsylvania Court of Common Pleas. I interviewed with her and a few other judges. In February 1976, Judge Harris offered me the position as her law clerk beginning in September. I was ecstatic. Judicial clerkships were very competitive, and I was glad to get one. I now had two job offers. I accepted the clerkship with Judge Harris. This was more than just a highly sought-after position; I was going to work for Judge Harris, a black woman. There were only two black women judges on the Court of Common Pleas in Pennsylvania: Judge Harris and Judge Juanita Kidd Stout. There were not any black women judges on any state appellate court or on any federal trial or appellate court in Pennsylvania. I didn't know any black women lawyers in Philadelphia well enough to call on for advice. The only black woman judge I had ever heard about was Judge Constance Baker Motley, who worked with Justice Thurgood Marshall on the Brown vs. Board of Education case. She was the first black woman appointed to the federal bench and that was in 1966, just 10 years earlier.

With a job in hand, the pressure of third-year law school was almost gone. All I wanted to do was graduate, prepare to take the dreaded Pennsylvania Bar Exam, and go to work.

Before I received any job offers, I had signed up for an interview with Reginald Haber Fellows. We called it Reggie for short. Similar to CLS, it was a legal services organization that represented poor and minority people in communities throughout the United States. I was selected for an interview. The day of the interview, Jeff, my study partner, and I were having lunch in the cafeteria. I noticed that there were four white, male students seated at a table in front of us. They kept turning around, looking at us, and whispering to each other. I asked Jeff, "What do you think that's about? Why are they looking back here at us?"

Jeff looked over at them and shrugged. "I'm sure if it's important to them, we'll find out sooner or later," he said.

The four students finished talking and began to leave the cafeteria. Arnold, one of the students with them, walked over to our table. I knew Arnold; first year we sat next to each other in class. We weren't friends but we nodded when we saw each other in the halls. Arnold said, "Hi, Jeff, Kathy. I see you got an interview with the Reggie representative this afternoon."

Arnold was very tall; he stood so close to the table that I had to stretch my neck and lean back to look into his eyes. Then I pushed back from the table. "Yeah, at two o'clock, why?" I asked.

"Well, I heard you got a job. In fact, I heard you got a clerkship. So why are you still interviewing?" Arnold asked.

I quickly looked over at Jeff and showed my surprise at Arnold's question. It felt as if every nerve in my body stood at attention as I loaded up to take Arnold's head off. But I waited and thought that maybe I misunderstood his question. I stared at Arnold for a long few seconds, just in case he wanted to rethink what he asked me. But he just stood there and waited for me to answer him. Again, I looked in Jeff's direction. An amused, slight smile crossed his face; he shook his head and waited for my response.

Incredulously, in a loud whisper, I said, "What?" That is what someone says to let a fool know that they should not have said whatever it is they just said. I didn't wait for Arnold to respond.

"Why do I have to explain anything to you or anyone else about who I am interviewing with? I saw your name on the list. You have an interview with the 'Reggie' representative too. I didn't take your interview. So that's not what you're worried about. Now hear this: I don't tell you who to interview with and you don't tell me. Any more questions?"

Arnold straightened up to his full height; large red blotches covered his face and neck. He stammered, backed away from the table, and said in an indignant tone, "Well, it's just that other people are trying to get jobs too."

"Oh! Good looking out! Where were you when those employers didn't give me an interview but selected you and your boys for an interview? You weren't concerned about equal job opportunities then, were you? You take care of your business and I'll take care of mine. I will take the job I want from the offers I get. And I am sure everybody will do the same. I have the same rights as everybody else around here."

Arnold turned and hurried away. I fumed. Jeff shook his head in disbelief. I gathered my books and ran to the ladies lounge to get myself together because I wasn't going to be late for my interview.

Villanova University Law School gave me an excellent legal education. But most of all, my law school experience taught me that some rules were written and available for all to see; others were hidden and reserved for those who knew the game or had the inside track. I learned to keep my eyes and ears open, because all the rules that I needed to succeed would be revealed. What I learned outside the classroom, and especially the lessons that Dad taught me, would be invaluable and were packed to go with a call-on-demand feature. All I had to do was to remember them and have the courage to use them.

Along the way guiding angels, dream carriers, passed me along from one caring, concerned heart to another. The power that predestined my path and my progress could not be thwarted by small-minded people committed to maintaining the status quo. I learned throughout my journey that the status quo often was the unnatural order of things.

17

The Day Arrived

May 1976, the day before graduation, I picked up my cap and gown early in the afternoon. The law school graduation was the next morning at 9 a.m., and the large graduation for the entire university was scheduled for the afternoon. I really didn't want to go to the large graduation, but Mom wanted me to go to everything.

"Look, we missed the last graduation. Your father and I want to see you walk in both graduations," she said.

"Alright, alright. I'll do it. But we're going to have to find parking spaces and walk…" I stopped trying to explain why we didn't need to go to both graduation ceremonies. The expression on Mom's face as she tilted her head to one side and put her hands on her hips made it clear to me that she didn't want to hear any of my complaints.

I smiled. Everyone in the family, even Dad, understood that when Mom made up her mind about something, there was no point in arguing with her. She was always getting on me about my facial expressions and the look in my eyes. Now I knew where I got it from.

Later that night, I was straightening up the living room in our apartment when I stepped on a large nail. I screamed.

Michael ran into the room. "What's the matter? What happened?"

I hopped over to the sofa, pulled the nail out, and blood oozed from the hole in my foot. Michael watched and grimaced as if he felt my pain. He ran and got a towel to wrap around my foot. "Come on, I'm taking you to the hospital."

"Oh, no, I am not going to the emergency room at this time of night. You know that they will keep me there all night. I am not going to be late or miss graduation. That's it!" I said.

"You probably need a tetanus shot. A doctor needs to look at that. Come on!"

"No! I am not going. Just get me some peroxide. I promise I'll go after graduation tomorrow, but not tonight. I can't."

Michael understood but he didn't like it. He put peroxide and a bandage on my throbbing foot and helped me get into bed. In the morning, he felt my forehead to see if I had a temperature. I tried to walk as normally as possible, but my foot really hurt. I went to the front door to get the newspaper and to see what the weather was like. I hoped Michael wasn't looking because I really just wanted to see if I could walk on my throbbing foot.

When I opened the front door, I was surprised to see Dad's car parked in front of the house next door. Mom and Dad were sitting in the car, and my mother-in-law and father-in-law were in their car parked behind them. I yelled, "Hey, what are y'all doing here?" We had planned to meet at the law school.

Mom looked out the car window and slowly waved to me with a big grin on her face. She knew I was surprised to see them. Dad got out of the car.

"Hey, how you doing? Me and your mother are here to make sure you don't miss this one," he said, trying to look serious as he stifled a grin.

Michael came to the door, and Mr. and Mrs. Lewis and Aunt Shirley got out of their car. We all laughed. I limped through both graduation ceremonies.

Mom prepared a small dinner party for the family and some close friends. This party was not nearly as large or elaborate as my college graduation party. She told everyone not to come until after the graduation. Later that night, after most of the guests were gone, Michael and I got ready to go home. Dad pulled me aside. He was sitting in his chair in a corner of the living room. He held what was left of the big cigar that he lit right after graduation and had puffed on all day. He said, "I knew you could do it. Me and your mother are proud of you."

He kissed me on the forehead. "All these people better get out of here now. I got to get up early to go to work in the morning."

All that I learned inside and outside the classroom helped me achieve my dream. Formal education within the walls of established school buildings had come to an end. But I knew my education was not over. I was stepping into a world with more rules, hidden agendas, and a status quo that did not expect me to become a lawyer. There were going to be many more tests and most would be unannounced.

* * *

However, the last and most important expected test after law school was the Pennsylvania Bar Exam. Dad's advice centered me as I prepared to get over this hurdle. Studying for the Bar Exam balled me up in knots. I planned my schedule: 8:30 a.m. to 5:30 p.m. I studied in a windowless room in the basement of Penn's law school, with a half-hour to eat the lunch I brought with me. Without windows, I was unaware of the time of day, and I kept my watch in my duffel bag. I intended to break for dinner and any other obligations at about 5:30 p.m., continue studying at 8 p.m. until bedtime. I reviewed my outlines and bar review course materials, and met with my informal study group for a couple of hours in the afternoon.

As I stuck to the plan, my tension increased. I needed a release, a way to step back, relax, and clear my mind just for a little while. This would help me to study better. One evening when Michael came home from work, I had washed all the windows in our apartment. It was the first time in the two years that we lived there that daylight came through the windows so clearly that we didn't need to turn a light on to see. Another time Michael came home and I had made a rum cake, which was beautifully decorated. Michael was shocked and at first didn't believe I made the cake. He hoped that this was a sign that I would start cooking meals that required more than 30 minutes from concept to table. For years he employed his best therapy techniques to get me interested in cooking. It didn't work on me but he became an excellent cook.

Finally, a month before the Bar Exam, Michael came home and saw a five-speed blue bicycle in the living room. He dropped his book bag on the floor and looked around the room and down the hallway to see if anyone was in the bathroom or the kitchen located in the rear of the apartment. He said, "Hi, Kathy, who's here? Whose bike is that?"

I was reading at my desk in the corner of the living room. I got up from the desk with a big smile and said, "Hi, it's mine; it's a five-speed. I placed a special order for it with Sears because I didn't want a ten-speed. I know that's what most people have."

Michael stared at the bike, his brow furrowed, and in an incredulous whisper he said, "But Kathy, you don't know how to ride a bike."

I sighed. "I know that. I want you to teach me."

"What? When? You've got to study. When are you going to learn to ride, after the exam? So why did you get a bike now?"

"I need a distraction to help me study better. I want to learn to ride. We can go to the park after you get home from work and ride before we have dinner. Will you teach me?"

"Uh, okay, but after I teach you, I'm going to buy a bike so we can ride together. Don't talk to me about the budget because I am not getting a five-speed bike."

Michael and I rode our bicycles for the rest of the summer, even after the Bar Exam. My father never allowed me to ride a bike growing up because he was afraid I'd get hurt. Also, he believed that riding bikes was for boys. Michael taught me to ride a bike at age 24. I learned the importance of balance when I wanted to do my best.

July 1976: the exam was at the end of the month, and I had studied every day for the last two months. A week before the exam, I studied one subject all day. At the end of the day, I met with my study group, which consisted of seven law students, a few who had graduated from Villanova University Law School with me and a couple who graduated from other law schools. Each of us studied alone in the morning and then we met in the afternoon to go over practice Bar Exam questions. That day during our group session, I got most of the answers wrong. I was so angry at myself, I couldn't think straight. It felt as if I was losing my mind. I kept asking myself, "What's the matter with you?" I went home and emotionally imploded as I threw things, paced the floor, and cried. I thought, This can't be happening; I've studied and I know this stuff. Am I going to blow this exam?

When I was all cried out, the pounding inside my head subsided. Physically and emotionally exhausted, I began to relax. I remembered what Dad told me so many times: "Control your emotions, don't let your emotions control you." I sat very still and just stared at a blank wall in the apartment. What was I doing wrong? A light went off inside me and I knew the answer: I was too uptight. I wasn't allowing what I knew to come out. I thought that if I fail this exam because I don't know the material, I can go back and study, learn it, take the exam again, and pass it. But if I fail because I can't control my emotions and show what I know, then I may never pass it.

Now I knew what I had to do. I got something to eat, took a nap, got up, and studied until time to go to bed. The next day, I followed my study routine and met with the study group.

October 1976, I received notice that I successfully passed the Pennsylvania Bar Examination on my first try.

Dad's mantras continue to provide me with life-sustaining food for thought and life preservers needed to take me through storms. I thank God that all the lessons I learned along the way were embedded within me. I benefited from them in the past, and I was sure that I was going to need them in the future. I stepped through the looking glass into the legal profession.

After graduation from Villanova University School of Law.

Kathryn Streeter Lewis, Esquire, enjoyed practicing law.

1988. I was sworn in as First Deputy Solicitor. On the left, James P. Lewis, father-in-law and a Montfort Point Marine. On the right, Mom and Dad—Margaret and John Streeter, always there for me.

PART III

PRESS ON

18

Not My Will

It wasn't until I crossed the finish lines that I realized this was just the beginning: I graduated from law school, passed the Pennsylvania Bar, and had a job. Now what?

Growing up, my goal was to be a criminal defense lawyer. It wasn't that I didn't like prosecutors; I just didn't know any. Juvenile gangs were prevalent throughout the city, and many of the boys in my neighborhood were caught up in the criminal justice system. Neither the boys who were defendants in criminal cases nor their relatives had anything good to say about prosecutors. For that matter, unless they "beat the case," they didn't have anything good to say about their lawyers either. No one spoke about lawyers involved in any other areas of law, so I set my sights on becoming a criminal defense lawyer. This choice required me to battle internal contradictions. I wanted to be an advocate and protect those in the neighborhood where I grew up. But there were times when some of the same young people that I wanted to defend undermined the peace and threatened the security of the people in the neighborhood that I wanted to protect. I had an affinity for the underdog, those whose rights were denied or disregarded with impunity. This ignited my desire to fight and had the greatest pull on my spirit.

After law school I was fortunate to be chosen by the Honorable Doris May Harris, a black woman and the first black woman judge I ever met, to serve as her law clerk. In 1976, she was assigned to the Family Court Division and presided over juvenile delinquency and domestic relations cases. Midway through my clerkship, Judge Harris asked about my plans for the future. I told her about my interest in criminal law and employment discrimination. She recommended that I apply to the District Attorney's Office. She was trying to guide me to a career path that would best advance my interest in criminal law and my entry into the profession. Generally, prosecutors were highly regarded. However, there were not many black prosecutors in the Philadelphia District Attorney's Office—the number could be counted on both hands—and only a couple were supervisors.

Judge Harris didn't know much about the gritty underbelly of my upbringing, such as what made me decide to become a lawyer, the people who I grew up with who had been killed, wounded, or incarcerated as a result of juvenile gang wars. As a black woman, Judge Harris understood very well my struggles to get to this point in my career but not what motivated my choices. I admired, respected, and valued her opinion, but I wasn't interested in applying to the District Attorney's Office. Instead I decided to apply to the Defender Association of Philadelphia, Community Legal Services (CLS) (I previously received a job offer from CLS when I was in law school), Pennsylvania Human Relations Commission, and the U.S. Equal Employment Opportunity Commission (EEOC).

The Public Defender Association was my first choice. I was excited when I was granted an interview. I appeared for the interview wearing my navy pinstriped suit, white starched blouse with a Peter Pan collar, and a cranberry and blue striped scarf bow tie. My black pumps were shined and matched my plain, no-designer-name handbag. I was still following the *Dress for Success* protocol. There were four attorneys on the interview panel, all white men. I extended my hand, looked each of them in the eye, and shook their hands firmly. That's how Dad taught me to introduce myself.

One of the men pointed to a seat across the table from them for me to sit down. I answered their questions for about 30 minutes. The interview seemed to be going pretty well.

Then one of the attorneys asked, "Have you or anyone in your family ever been a victim of a violent crime?"

I could have given a list of people, but the first person who came to mind was my younger sister Reese, who had been stabbed repeatedly when she was 13 years old. I told them about the incident and that it occurred when I was a second-year law student. The interviewers listened in silence; one fidgeted in his seat, another's jaw dropped. They had not anticipated my response. This was much more than the usual stories about the gang that jumped my brother and beat him up, somebody stole our porch furniture, or the guy who shot my dad during an attempt to rob him as he left a takeout restaurant in the neighborhood. All of these things also happened to members of my family, but that was run-of-the-mill stuff, life on the streets, in the ghetto of North Philadelphia. No need to mention any of that.

Two attorneys, neither of whom had asked the question, inquired about the details of the crime and if anyone had been arrested. I told them no one was arrested. Then the attorney who asked the first question said, "If you worked here and were assigned to represent one of the guys who did that to your sister, could you represent him?"

I stared at him, now keenly aware of his disheveled hair, slightly wrinkled shirt, and Coke-bottle-thick, dark-frame glasses. He looked at me intently and waited for an answer. I thought he expected me to say yes, that I could represent anyone who I was assigned to represent. I guessed that that was what a tough, "bad-ass" criminal defense lawyer might say. I also knew that there were a lot of reasons why I would never be given such an assignment. I answered honestly. "No, it would be better if someone else was assigned to represent him."

The lawyer went into a tirade. He shouted, "Don't you

know that everyone is entitled to a defense? As a criminal defense lawyer, it's not your job to decide guilt or innocence. You defend your client. You're supposed to do your damned job! You're not fit to be a criminal defense lawyer."

I remained still as he ranted. As I listened to him, I recalled the vicious attack on my sister and how it affected our family. I felt the fire of anger roaring to the surface, but suddenly a peace settled over me. When he finished, I took a deep breath and attempted to explain that I knew everyone was entitled to a defense, but I couldn't represent the person who did that to my "baby sister." He rolled his eyes and turned his back to me. Another attorney in the room put an end to the tension that had polluted the air and thanked me for coming. The interview ended. A few days later, I received a letter thanking me for my interest, but no job offer.

* * *

Twenty-five years later I crossed paths again with that attorney who berated me and closed the door to the career path that I chose for myself. I was the judge assigned to preside over a homicide case and he represented the defendant. During a pretrial conference, I listened carefully as he and the assistant district attorney presented their arguments. At the conclusion of the pretrial conference, I took the matter under advisement. As the defendant's attorney prepared to leave the courtroom, he closed his briefcase, looked up at me seated on the bench, and said, "Have a good day, Your Honor." I smiled as I remembered the last time when we sat across from each other. His tone and demeanor were very different this time. Twenty-five years ago, perhaps he was partially right when he said that I wasn't "fit to be a criminal defense lawyer." Neither he nor I had any idea that I would become a judge and preside over criminal cases. I don't know if he even remembered when we first met. I didn't tell him and I certainly wasn't holding any grudges. He did me a favor, and neither of us knew it at the time.

* * *

Early spring of 1977, rejected by the Public Defender's Office, my first choice, the search for my next job continued. My clerkship was only for one year and ended at the end of August. The Pennsylvania Human Relations Commission offered me a job, but I had to decline because they wanted me to start before my clerkship ended. The federal government had a freeze on hiring. The general counsel at EEOC told me they were interested in making me an offer, but they couldn't do any hiring until the freeze was lifted. A few months before the end of my clerkship, CLS offered me a position as a staff attorney beginning September 1977. At last the pressure was off, I found a job.

Judge Harris took vacation in August and closed the office. What a great job! First year out of law school and one month paid vacation. Lucy, the judge's secretary, was glad to have a month vacation, but she complained about all the mail and work that piled up when the office was closed.

The third week of my vacation, I decided to go into the office to sort the mail and handle anything that I could before the judge and Lucy returned from vacation. I knew that I didn't have to, but Judge Harris had been a great mentor and boss and I wanted to help.

As I went through the mountain of mail that had accumulated, I received a call from William Hall, regional counsel of the Department of Housing and Urban Development (HUD). I worked at HUD as a summer intern after my first year in law school. He said that the executive director of the Philadelphia Council for Community Advancement (PCCA), a nonprofit agency that developed low- and moderate-income family housing, called him yesterday. He told Mr. Hall that PCCA was looking for a staff attorney and asked if he could recommend anyone. Mr. Hall said that he thought this was a great opportunity and wanted to recommend me for the position. I was glad that I came into the office that day. I moved since the time I worked for Mr. Hall at HUD. If I had not come into the office, he probably wouldn't have reached me.

"Yes. Thank you for thinking of me."

Mr. Hall gave me the name of the executive director, W. Wilson Goode, and his telephone number. He told me to call Mr. Goode and let him know that he told me to call. I called as soon as I got off the phone. Mr. Goode said that he planned to make a decision very soon and had narrowed his search to two candidates.

"Can you come in this afternoon at three?" he asked.

It was almost 1 p.m. then. "Yes, I'll be there."

I was glad that I wore a dress to the office, but I needed to buy some shoes and pantyhose. I had not planned to go to an interview and I was not in my best *Dress for Success* attire. I didn't have time to go home and change, but I couldn't go to an interview with bare feet in sandals.

I arrived for the interview on time, and it lasted almost an hour and a half. Mr. Goode told me about the agency, projects they were working on, and what he expected from a staff attorney. He gave me some brochures about projects that PCCA had completed and proposals concerning projects in progress. At the end of our meeting, Mr. Goode said, "Read this information and call me tomorrow if you think you might be interested in the position."

That evening I read the information and was very interested in PCCA's projects and excited about the opportunity to be the agency's staff attorney. I called Mr. Goode the next day. "I am interested in the position but I have a few questions."

"Tomorrow is Sunday; can you come in about two o'clock? We can talk more then."

"I'll be there."

We met and talked for about 45 minutes. After he

answered my questions, he told me the salary, which was less than what CLS offered me and much less than a position at EEOC, if the freeze was lifted. He said he expected the agency's funding to increase next year and then he would be able to increase the salary. The doorbell rang. He had another meeting scheduled and people began to arrive.

"I want to offer you the position. Think about it. Call me on Monday and let me know if you'll accept. I intend to fill the position this week. Thanks for coming in," he said.

That evening I discussed the position with Michael and Dad. When I spoke to Dad, he asked, "Which job pays the most between PCCA and CLS?"

I told him CLS paid more.

"If you can still take the job with the federal government after the freeze is lifted, that would be my first choice. It pays more money than both of the other jobs. Government jobs have good benefits and are pretty secure," Dad said.

Later that evening Michael and I discussed what I should do.

"You went to law school to be able to do what you want to do. Take the job you think you'll like best," Michael said.

Dad's advice wasn't bad, but it was colored by his life experiences and desire to provide for my long-term security. Opportunities for women and African Americans were evolving. The changes were new for both of us. My dream to become a lawyer was to be an advocate and help people. At 25 years old, a good salary was very important to me, but I wasn't really thinking about long-term security. As Dad and I looked into the prism-like looking-glass to decide my future, we had different perspectives. But I remembered one of his often-quoted Streeterisms: "The aggressor wins nine times out of ten."

In August 1977, I accepted the position of staff attorney for PCCA. My areas of specialty were real estate development, first-time homeowner counseling, and management of low- and moderate-income housing developments. Today, I still ride through Philadelphia and see housing developments that I worked on with neighborhood community groups. I remember how good it felt to watch as families moved into their first homes and to see community leaders beam with pride as they witnessed many years of hard work to improve the community come to fruition.

In 1978, Mr. Goode was appointed by the governor of Pennsylvania to serve on the Pennsylvania Public Utility Commission and ultimately became the chairman of the Commission. About seven months after his appointment, Mr. Goode called and asked if I would consider serving as his staff counsel. I was reluctant because I didn't know anything about public utility law. However, I knew that getting utility companies to cooperate in providing utility service for many of PCCA's projects was a recurring problem. Also, the job would require me to work in Harrisburg, which was 90 miles away from Philadelphia. All of my activities, friends, and family were in Philadelphia, and I wasn't about to move. Harrisburg was the capital of Pennsylvania, and many professionals commuted there from Philadelphia. Commuting to and from Harrisburg every day would definitely put me out of the loop in Philadelphia, professionally and socially.

Before I made a decision, Mr. Goode asked me to come to Harrisburg and observe the Public Utility Commission in session at a public meeting. I agreed. I met him and his assistant, Bob, at 5:30 a.m. in the parking lot of a shopping center on City Avenue. Mr. Goode left for Harrisburg every day at 5:30 a.m. because he wanted to arrive at the office by 7:15 a.m., before his staff arrived at 8 a.m.

I attended the public meeting and watched as the Commission presided over matters that affected utility service throughout Pennsylvania, which included setting rates for all privately-owned public utility and transportation companies, resolving customer service disputes, and issuing rules and regulations. Attorneys began presenting cases in the morning and the hearings did not end until mid-afternoon. I noticed that there were not any women or minority attorneys representing any of the parties involved.

After the public meeting, I approached the chief counsel for the Public Utility Commission. "Hello, I am here today observing the proceedings and I noticed that there weren't any women or African American attorneys involved in any of the cases before the Commission. Is that unusual?" I asked.

Without looking up from his files on the table, he said, "No."

Undeterred by his obvious intent not to have a conversation with me, I asked him another question. "Why do you think women and African Americans don't handle these types of cases?"

He quickly continued putting his files in a large litigation briefcase, fastened it, and glanced in my direction. "I guess it's just too technical for them," he said. Then he turned and walked away.

The words reverberated in my head. I recalled what he said over and over again: "Just too technical for them."

I went back to Mr. Goode's office. He asked what I thought about the work that went on at the Commission.

"It's very interesting. I'll take the job," I said. I could see that he was surprised by how quickly I responded.

"Uh, fine. Let me know how soon you can start. If you want, you can ride to Harrisburg with me and Bob, but you know that I leave at five-thirty in the morning, or you can take the six o'clock train, it gets here before eight," he said.

He didn't ask what convinced me to take the job and I didn't volunteer. But I had to know what about this work was "too technical" for women and African Americans. My new area of practice would be public utility law. In the evenings, I met frequently with community groups that wanted to develop low- and moderate-income housing in their neighborhoods and shared with them how the Public Utility Commission operated. I told them what they needed to do to get utility companies to cooperate in the development process and how to file consumer complaints.

* * *

As I look back on the plan I had for my career, now I know that there was a better plan. I am forever grateful that my future was not determined by the extent of my knowledge, at a time when I was unaware of how little I knew. I learned that there were many areas of law that had an impact on the lives of people who I wanted to help. I have been blessed to appreciate how much more abundant life can be when it's not limited by my will.

19

Don't Get Pushed Around

Glad to be back. I commuted to Harrisburg for almost two years. I kept in touch as best I could with what was going on in Philly in the legal community and the black community. The political landscape was in flux; the second formidable black candidate for mayor, Charles Bowser, Esq., lost the Democratic primary after an impressive challenge. Congressman William J. Green was elected mayor and named W. Wilson Goode managing director of the City of Philadelphia. I applied and was hired as an assistant city solicitor in the Law Department for the City of Philadelphia. I was assigned to the Energy and Utilities Unit and served as counsel to the Philadelphia Gas Commission, which governed the management of the Philadelphia Gas Works (PGW). When I worked at the Pennsylvania Public Utility Commission (PUC), there were always complaints from PGW customers. But the PUC didn't have jurisdiction over PGW because it was owned by the city.

In the fall of 1980, advocates for gas customers in Philadelphia asked the city to order PGW to cease terminations of gas service during the winter. Managing Director Goode suggested to the city solicitor that he assign me to develop policies and procedures to prevent termination of gas service for customers unable to pay during the winter months. At the PUC I was on a task force that developed Cold Weather Interim Procedures to protect the elderly, those seriously ill, and families with young children who were unable to pay from having their utility services terminated during the winter months. The Commission implemented the procedures. Managing Director Goode wanted a similar program in Philadelphia for PGW, and he wanted me to work with the Gas Commission to develop it. The city solicitor assigned me to work with the Gas Commission to develop winter termination procedures for PGW.

I knew this wasn't going to be easy. I was recently assigned as counsel to the Commission. I was not yet 30 years old, less than five years out of law school, and a black woman. I didn't share any of these characteristics with anyone on the Gas Commission or in PGW's senior management. PGW's management resisted any attempt to interfere with what had been its unfettered right to terminate service during the winter under any circumstances. I submitted several drafts of proposed procedures to the Commission for its approval. PGW's management vehemently opposed all of them. They insisted that most of the customers threatened with termination of service had the ability to pay and were just deadbeats. And the only way to get them to pay was to cut off service when they needed it most, during the dead of winter.

In response I recommended that the Gas Commission hold termination hearings during the day and after work to permit customers to come in with proof of income and explain why their service should not be terminated. If someone had the ability to pay, they were ordered to do so. Anyone who was unable to pay was permitted to enter into a payment agreement based on their financial circumstances, and service would not be shut off. PGW's customer service staff found other resources for households with seriously ill or disabled adults, or with very young children, who were unable to pay for service which prevented service terminations. Pre-termination hearings were not the norm. The Gas

Commissioners presided at the hearings, which were held during the day and in the evenings. PGW's management and staff were required to be present and prepared to enter into agreements with customers.

When the first hearings were held, I was six months pregnant. Until I went out on maternity leave, I attended every hearing; some lasted late into the night. Customers filled the hearing room and appreciated a chance to be heard. Many enjoyed acting as their own attorney and arguing their case before the Commission. Some were too nervous to present the documents they brought or explain their circumstances. The Commission staff assisted them.

PGW's management, who vehemently opposed the recommended procedures and hearings, especially the ones held in the evenings, ultimately came around. They saw that I listened, even as I pushed forward to accomplish the objective, and addressed their concerns, if possible. The program was successfully implemented and well underway when I went out on maternity leave. The city and PGW were commended for taking steps to prevent deaths as a result of service terminations during the winter.

* * *

The winter of 1981, our son, Michael, was born; he added a wonderful, fulfilling dimension to our family. Michael and I decided to give him my maiden name, Streeter, as his middle name. Dad always said the reason fathers wanted sons was to carry on the family name. My brother, Johnny, had a daughter, Chereese, and now I had a son who carried the family name. My son carried the name of the two men who meant the most to me. As I prepared to return to work, Michael and I had to create another new normal, which included parenting and professional responsibilities.

Spring 1981, a couple of months after I returned from maternity leave, the city solicitor, Alan J. Davis, called me to his office and said that he was considering assigning me to the Housing Unit. The Housing Unit was responsible for the city's publicly funded housing and community-based economic development programs. I was told that the executive director of the Housing Unit, Gregory Coleman, had requested that a different attorney be assigned to the unit. I was surprised and excited that Alan was considering me for the position.

* * *

I remembered the last time I met with Alan one to one. It was after the doctor told me I was pregnant. For weeks I rehearsed in my head what I wanted to say to Alan. I didn't want to be written off or not taken seriously about my intention to be a lawyer. I was married for six years and graduated from law school four years ago. Why did I have to choose between becoming a mother and working as a lawyer? I made an appointment to meet with Alan to tell him I was pregnant, and my plan to continue working until I had the baby and to return to work after the baby was born.

When I entered his office, he greeted me with a warm smile, stood up, came from behind his desk, and shook my hand as we sat in armchairs in front of his desk. He asked me how things were going in the Utility Unit and expressed approval with how I handled setting up PGW's winter termination procedures. I liked Alan. He was smart, highly respected, and principled. I saw him interact with others in the office and watched him answer questions in staff meetings. He listened, was direct, and tried to be fair. It was my turn to tell him why I asked to meet with him.

"Mr. Davis—"

"Kathy, please call me Alan, everybody else does." He smiled and his eyes twinkled.

I took a deep breath. I wondered if he would still be so warm and approachable after I told him why I was there.

"Okay, Alan, I recently found out that I'm pregnant. I'm due in March. I plan to come back to work six weeks after the baby is born. I want to know if I'll be able to get my job back?"

His eyes opened wide. "Well, congratulations. I am happy for you and your husband."

He waved his hand in the way someone does when the question didn't need to be asked.

"Look, you don't need to worry about your job. You'll have a position in this office. If I'm here, you have a place here, and I don't plan on going anywhere anytime soon. Now, I don't know if I'll need to assign someone to the Utilities Unit while you're out. But don't worry about that. If that spot is open, it's yours. If not, there will be something else in the office. I'm sure of it. Now, you don't have to commit to a date when you'll return. Take whatever time you need. Some women decide not to go back to work until their children start school. Take your time and let us know when you're ready to come back. Good luck to you."

I felt better. The idea of staying home until my child went to school was farfetched. I didn't know any black women who had children, and a job to go back to, who didn't go back to work until their children went to school. Mr. Davis and I didn't share the same reality about such things. But he removed a burden from my mind. I believed him and trusted him to keep his word. I came back to work eight weeks after our son, Michael, was born.

* * *

After Alan told me about the position in the Housing Unit, I called Robert Paul, the divisional deputy assigned to the unit, and asked to meet with him. He was reluctant to tell me much about the legal matters the unit handled. In fact, he spent most of the time telling me about his extensive housing experience and asking me questions about my experience. It was obvious that he was trying to discourage me or at least make me think that this assignment was more than I could handle.

Later that afternoon, I met with Mr. Coleman, the executive director. He was friendly, professional, and made no secret that lawyers assigned to the Housing Unit were essential to the programs he planned to implement. Mr. Coleman was very intelligent, confident, and knew how to get things done. We talked generally about housing needs in the city, neighborhood community groups, and government regulations for spending federal funds. Afterwards, Mr. Coleman asked if I had any questions. Then he sat back in his chair behind a large desk that separated us. He was quiet for a few minutes and looked at me intently before he said, "I need a lawyer to solve problems, not just find them. And I need a lawyer who gets things done timely." He wasn't smiling anymore.

Now I understood what he found lacking in his current counsel. He had been told about my experience in the development and management of low- and moderate-income housing when I worked for the Philadelphia Council for Community Advancement. He was willing to give me a chance, if I was interested and understood what he expected.

A few days later the city solicitor announced that I would replace Mr. Paul as the deputy assigned to the Housing Unit. For the first time I would supervise a staff of attorneys, a paralegal, and two secretaries. Along with the promotion I received a 10 percent salary increase. Several attorneys in the office congratulated me; others didn't acknowledge my promotion.

Later that afternoon, after the announcement, a woman attorney in the office approached me in the ladies room. She said that she heard I was only going to be promoted to a deputy city solicitor but that my predecessor was a divisional deputy city solicitor, which paid much more than "just a deputy."

"If I was you, I wouldn't take the job unless they paid me the same as the man you're going to replace. It's just not right," she said.

I thought about what she said. As a woman I should be paid as much as a man if I am to do the job he was hired to do. I appreciated her perspective, but I was reminded of lessons Dad taught me: *Don't let anybody build a bridge over your nose. Think for yourself.* This woman had never sought to be a mentor, advocate, or, for that matter, befriend me since I came to work in the office. Now here she was telling me what she would do. But more to the point, what I shouldn't do. Why was she telling me this? It certainly mattered to me that I not become a victim of racism or sexism. Was this promotion a manifestation of either? There was only one other African American woman supervisor in the office. How would my rejecting this position because of the pay difference advance race or gender equality? The city solicitor was taking a gamble on me. It was a significant position, and there were many white attorneys with more seniority in the office than I had, even if they didn't have my housing experience. To reject the position because I was not being promoted to the same position as my predecessor may have been perceived by some people as a bold statement. But it didn't seem to be a wise decision. I decided to take the promotion and not make an issue about the salary or the job title.

The day after the announcement was made, Robert called me. He said that there were a number of things that he wanted to finish before he left the unit. I was told that he was assigned to another unit in the Law Department in a non-supervisory position at the same salary. He told me that he had set up a table for me in the corner of his office and that I could use it for the next couple of weeks. He expected to complete some things he needed to do by then, and then he would move to his new unit. I didn't like this table-in-the-corner arrangement, but I knew he was upset about being replaced. I didn't protest; I planned to work from my current office until he left.

A couple of days later, he called and asked me to come meet with him and the staff to go over some pending projects and to get an orientation about how the office operated. I wanted to know about pending projects, but I really wasn't interested in an operational strategy that resulted in his demise. I went to the meeting. Within 15 minutes after I arrived, Robert said that something had come up that he needed to take care of and he would be back soon. He insisted that I stay and meet with the staff until he got back. I stayed for about an hour. Robert didn't return.

I went back to my office, which was across the street in the building where the Law Department was located. I ran into Robert as he was getting off the elevator in the building where I worked. "Hey, what happened to you? I thought you were coming back. There are some things we need to discuss," I said.

He quickly glanced in my direction. Looking straight ahead, without breaking his stride, he said abruptly, "Yeah, I got held up. We can schedule another time."

He left the building.

I took the elevator to the 15th floor and headed toward my office. First Deputy Solicitor, Carl Singley, came up the hall and called out to me. "Kathy, you should know that Robert just left Alan's office. He asked to meet with Alan and suggested that he keep his position and that you be assigned to work for him. Alan told him no, the decision had been made, and he expected Robert to help you with a smooth transition."

That snake! He wanted me out of the building so he could sneak over here to meet with Alan. Now I was pissed off.

"I just came from his office. He arranged for me to meet with him and the staff. And then he left."

"Kathy, that guy wants to keep his position. Watch your back." He laughed and got on the elevator.

I went to my office and began cleaning out my desk. I had only been back from maternity leave a couple of months, so I didn't have a lot of files or stuff to move. I called the maintenance staff and asked if they could move my things across the street to the Housing Unit that afternoon. They said they would come to my office after lunch. Next, I called Robert.

"Hey, Robert, I just got off the phone with the guys in maintenance and asked if they could move my things to my new office this afternoon. They should get there about three o'clock. If you have anything that you want to send to your new office, you should have it ready for them to take away," I said nonchalantly.

"What?" His surprise was obvious. "You were just here. You saw that I'm not anywhere near packed up. I'm going to need at least a week or so. You and I still need to meet to go over some things."

Robert was speaking hurriedly, shocked by my impending occupancy and his immediate eviction.

"Well, you can put your stuff on that table you set up in the office for me. I'll let you know when we can meet. I'll be over to put my stuff away later." I didn't wait for a response. This was not a negotiation. I hung up.

* * *

The next day, I arrived early to my new office ready to get to work. Robert was there when I arrived. Obviously annoyed, he quickly threw his things in boxes and moved out. We never had a transition meeting. Over the next month I met with all the managers in the Housing Unit in order to understand their duties and what they needed from the attorneys in my unit. I restructured the office and developed procedures to respond timely to matters assigned to the unit. After the first year in my new position, the executive director let the city solicitor know that things were going very well and he was pleased with my work.

Before the annual performance evaluations, I was offered the position of general counsel with a local nonprofit housing agency. The executive director, Julia O. Robinson, had been the deputy director of Housing and we had worked on many projects together. I told her I would think about it.

I met with the managing attorney in the Law Department assigned to supervise the Housing Unit.

"Kathy, we've heard very good things about your work and how you've turned that office around. I am pleased to tell you that I am going to recommend that you receive a salary increase of eight to ten percent. The executive committee is working on the budget for next year. You should know that the across-the-board increase will be much less than that, but I feel your work warrants an above-average increase." He smiled and I could tell he expected me to be pleased and to thank him.

Even with another 10 percent increase, my salary would still be less than what my predecessor earned. I nodded slowly. "I know that I was paid a lot less than Robert when I was assigned to replace him. But now that I've demonstrated that I can do the job that he didn't do, I should be paid what the job was worth when you hired him," I said.

The managing attorney's brow furrowed; he sat back in his chair and his face turned red. "Uh, Ka..., Kathy, you can appreciate that a twenty percent salary increase in a one-year period is very substantial."

I nodded and sat quietly for a few moments. "But it is not equal to what Robert was paid."

Then I told him that I had another job offer, but I did not want to give them an answer until after I spoke to him. He promised to get back to me in a few days after he spoke with Alan.

Late the next afternoon, the managing attorney called me. "Kathy, I spoke to Alan. You will be promoted to a divisional deputy and paid the same salary as your predecessor. We look forward to you remaining with the Law Department."

I learned to ask for what I deserve. But it's important to know when to ask and to be prepared to take action if I don't get it.

20

The Final Hurdle

In 1985, the legal community in Philadelphia was reeling as a result of accusations of judges taking cash in return for giving litigants favorable treatment. Demands to change how judges were selected and vetted before running for, or being appointed to, the bench was in the news every week. Even before news of the scandals, the Bar Association implemented a Judicial Selection and Retention Commission to screen judicial candidates. There was an urgent need to fill the vacancies quickly, but demand for more intense scrutiny was not going away. In response to the uproar, Governor Robert Casey appointed a commission, the Ryan Commission, to review candidates seeking to be appointed to the court. The Ryan Commission, which included attorneys, community and business leaders (both men and women), and representatives from every major minority group in the city, reviewed applications, conducted background investigations, interviewed candidates, and recommended a list of candidates to the governor. The governor committed to fill judicial vacancies from a list of candidates recommended by the Ryan Commission and approved by the Bar Association's Judicial Selection Commission.

After working as an attorney for 12 years, the thought of becoming a judge was not on my radar until a few of my friends suggested it. As luck or misfortune would have it, depending on your perspective, 10 judges had been removed from the bench as a result of a federal investigation into judicial corruption. In 1986, the Ryan Commission, with white-glove boldness, ventured into the bare-knuckle political landscape that previously controlled all elected offices in the city. Selection of "qualified judges" was the stated objective of the competing processes, but tight-fisted control of the process was the real prize. Five candidates recommended to the governor by the Commission ran and were elected over the political parties' endorsed slate of candidates.

Even with the election of the "Casey 5," as they were called, entrenched political leaders were not willing to relinquish power or control of the judicial selection process to the governor, the Ryan Commission, or the Bar Association. But the scandal, which continued to dominate the headlines, made business as usual no longer a viable option. A tenuous spirit of cooperation among the competing players resulted. There was legitimate concern that the new processes not undermine the appointment and election of minorities and women to the bench.

The first black mayor, W. Wilson Goode, was elected in 1983, and three black judges were elected to the Court of Common Pleas. In 1987, Philadelphia was the fifth largest city in the United States, with a population of almost 1.5 million people. There were 80 judges on the Court of Common Pleas; only six were women, and four of them had served less than five years. There were three black women and no Asian or Hispanic women. It was hoped that the governor's decision to create a diverse commission to recommend candidates to fill judicial vacancies would address this disparity.

I was appointed first deputy city solicitor after Mayor Goode was re-elected in 1987. I applied for the position of city solicitor but the mayor selected another candidate, the former chancellor of the Bar Association. The *Philadelphia Tribune*, the oldest African American newspaper in the United States, published an angry editorial when I was not selected for the position.

I was in my new position for a few months when some friends suggested that I seek an appointment to the Common Pleas Court. When the idea was suggested, my plate was full. I was representing the city in its effort to build a new convention center which would incorporate the Reading Terminal Train Shed, a historic landmark, and include an adjoining major hotel. I was also involved in several major development projects throughout the city.

But the thought of becoming a judge sparked my curiosity. I was well aware that this was still very much a political process, now being played out in several arenas. It reminded me of a childhood game called "steal the bacon." A stick represents the bacon and players line up on opposite sides to see who could grab the bacon and run back to their side. The team that grabs the bacon without being tagged by an opposing player wins. Players approach the bacon at the same time, then a strategic dance begins to see who could move the fastest, distract or outmaneuver their opponent, and grab the prize. To capture an appointment to fill a vacancy on the court was the bacon, and there were opposing players on many sides.

I had worked with players on all sides. My work brought me in contact with elected and appointed officials regularly. I was active in the Barristers Association, the minority bar association, a member of the Philadelphia and Pennsylvania Bar Associations, active in church and community organizations. But I was neither a political operative nor a "bar fly." I did not summarily reject my friends' suggestion that I throw my hat in the ring for a judicial appointment. The advice that Dr. McKay, my high school guidance counselor, gave me in 12th grade came to mind as fiercely as the day she got in my face when I was reluctant to apply to the University of Pennsylvania. "Don't you write yourself off. If you want something, you apply and go after it…" That's what she told me nearly 20 years ago.

I called Judge Higginbotham to ask his advice. We usually met over lunch in his chambers or in the court cafeteria a couple times a year to discuss my career and to keep in touch. I told him I was interested in a judgeship and about the new selection process.

"Kathy, I think you would be a great judge. You should definitely apply."

I shared my concerns about the process, which required that I receive the Ryan Commission's recommendation and the Bar Association's approval. It was not stated publicly, but any candidate who expected to run citywide and get elected would need one or more political sponsors.

"Your credentials and experience are excellent. What you should be prepared to address are concerns that some people will raise about your age. Compared to most of us old-timers on the bench, you're still pretty young." He laughed in that high-pitched laugh that was as much his trademark as his deep baritone voice and scholarly intellect. "How old are you?"

"Thirty-four."

"If you get appointed, I think that you would be one of the youngest judges on the bench," he said.

"Do you think that I'm too young to apply?" I asked.

"No, I don't. You need to let anyone who questions your ability because of your age know that wisdom does not always come with age, and one's ability should not be measured solely by that criteria. Then talk about your background and wealth of experience."

I left the judge's chambers almost certain that I would apply. There was still a major obstacle that I had to consider. I spoke to my friend Jimmie Moore, an attorney who was politically astute. We graduated from law school at the same time, and he took my place as staff attorney at PCCA when I went to work for the PUC. I spoke to Julia Robinson; she was now the director of housing and a member of the mayor's cabinet. Julia was one of my closest friends, the big sister I never had. I met with Jimmie and Julia separately. The first question I asked each of them, "Do you think that I should apply to fill a vacancy on the Municipal Court, a court of limited jurisdiction with a six-year term of office, or the Court of Common Pleas, the court of general jurisdiction with a ten-year term?" Without hesitation they both advised me to apply for a seat on the Court of Common Pleas. Then I shared with them my greatest concern, the one that was holding me back.

"If I get appointed, in less than a year, I'll have to run for election to keep my seat on the bench. Citywide elections are expensive and I'll need to raise a lot of money. If I don't raise enough money, I can't run an effective campaign. Where am I going to get that kind of money from? And if I lose the election, I'll be out of a job," I said.

I had spoken with a few judges who ran before and asked how they raised money to finance their campaigns. They told me that they used their savings and raised money from family and friends mostly. Some mortgaged their homes or borrowed money from banks, loans that some were still paying back. I couldn't afford to do this. Jimmie and Julia both said, "Don't worry about the money. If you get appointed, you'll raise the money you need to get elected."

I felt like I did when I was a little girl in the schoolyard playing "Double Dutch," a jump-rope game. The rope would be turning as I rocked back and forth, trying to decide when, and in this case if, I should to jump in.

When I told Dad about my financial worry, he said, "I'm not a rich man, but me and your mother will help you. I got a little money saved. Don't worry about it."

Michael knew what was holding me back from going for a seat on the bench. "Don't worry about the money. You can do this and we will do whatever we have to do to raise the money," he said.

"Look, I am not going to mortgage our house or—" I

wanted to discourage him from thinking about anything drastic. He cut me off.

"Kathy, don't worry about stuff before it happens. That probably won't be necessary anyway."

I submitted my applications to the Ryan Commission and to the Bar Association's Judicial Selection and Retention Commission. I received a rating of "Recommended" from the Philadelphia Bar Association.

In February 1987, I appeared for an interview before the Ryan Commission. The large conference room was filled. I recognized a few faces of lawyers I knew from Bar Association activities, community and business leaders involved in various projects I worked on over the years. I was asked questions about my background, answers to questions on my application, and other general questions. They asked if I was prepared and willing to run for election, if I was appointed to fill one of the vacancies. Then a member of the Commission asked the question that I sensed that they saved for last.

"Your credentials are impressive, but you know that if you are appointed to the bench, there will be many demands placed on you personally and professionally. Your activities will be restricted. You understand that you will be a judge on and off the bench, and as a result you will be expected to avoid even the appearance of impropriety. Have you thought about that?"

While the question did not directly ask if I was ready to take on this significant responsibility at my age, I knew that's what they wanted to know. I was 34 years old, younger than the judges currently on the bench and most of the other applicants. I attempted to assure them that I understood the duties and responsibilities of a judge on and off the bench. I also sought to paraphrase, albeit not as eloquently, what Judge Higginbotham said to me when he told me to anticipate concerns about my age.

"I have been told that one should not assume that with age

comes wisdom or that with youth comes immaturity or poor judgement," I said in response to the question.

I explained that in my current position, I had a great deal of responsibility and that my integrity and upbringing motivated me to avoid the appearance of impropriety in my personal and professional life.

A few days after the interview, I received a telephone call from a member of the Commission.

"You had a very good interview, and we were pleased to have the opportunity to meet you. There are so many outstanding candidates, which is good, which makes our job even more difficult. We regret that the Commission is not going to recommend you to the governor for consideration to fill a vacancy on the court. Thank you for your interest."

I sat back in my chair and let disappointment wash over me. After a few minutes, all the time allotted for my pity party, Phyllis, my secretary, buzzed me on the intercom to remind me that I had a meeting in 10 minutes. Quickly, I called Michael to let him know that I was rejected. He wanted to know all the details and at the same time tried to reassure me.

"Hey, I'm alright. I'll talk to you when I get home. I have to go to a meeting now."

After the meeting, I called Jimmie and Julia and told them the Commission's decision. That evening I called Dad.

Late March of 1988, I received a call from an attorney in the city who I knew to be politically connected and active in the Bar Association. He told me that he was aware that I had appeared before the Ryan Commission last year. He said there were still a few vacancies and he thought that I should reapply.

"Why do you think that?" I asked.

"I think you would be a good candidate and you've got a good shot at getting nominated. A lot of people were very surprised that the Commission did not select you. Just think about it."

Again, my friends and most trusted advisors urged me to reapply.

"Why? They said 'no.' I'm pretty smart. I know what 'no' means," I said.

My advisors pushed back. They told me that the word on the street was that my application was rejected because a few members of the Commission thought that I was too young to be a judge.

In April, I updated my application and resubmitted it. I appeared before the Commission for another interview, answered more questions, and waited to hear from them. A week later the call came.

"Hello, Mrs. Lewis. This time I am pleased to tell you that you have been approved by the Commission, and we will recommend you to the governor for consideration to fill a vacancy on the Court of Common Pleas. Good luck."

"Thank you. Thank you very much."

I wondered if my age had anything to do with the Commission's decision. I was rejected at age 34 and now recommended at age 36. That's what happened between February 1987 and May 1988, with a birthday in April.

First I called Michael, next Dad, and then each of my advisors. Now I waited to see if the governor would select me from the list of recommended candidates. Even if the governor nominated me, I'd still have go before the Pennsylvania Senate and be confirmed by a two-thirds vote. This was uncharted waters for me.

In 1987, Governor Robert Casey appointed Judge Juanita Kidd Stout to serve on the Pennsylvania Supreme Court. She was the first African American woman to serve on a court of record in Pennsylvania and now the first on the Pennsylvania Supreme Court. In 1969, when I graduated from high school, she was the first African American woman elected to the Court of Common Pleas in Pennsylvania. Judge Stout had a long and distinguished career on the Court of Common Pleas. She was a good friend of Judge Doris Harris when I clerked for her. I admired Justice Stout and enjoyed many conversations with her in the law library or when we attended conferences and other events. She always reached out to young attorneys with advice and encouragement.

Mid-May 1988, I received a telephone call. My secretary, Phyllis, answered the phone and placed the caller on hold. She was so excited, instead of using the intercom she ran into my office and, in a loud whisper, said, "It's the governor's office on the phone for you!"

I answered the phone. I am sure the man told me his name and position, but all I remember was what he said next. "Hello, Kathryn. I'm calling to tell you that the governor is going to nominate you to fill the vacancy on the Court of Common Pleas created as a result of Judge Juanita Kidd Stout's appointment to the Pennsylvania Supreme Court. There will be a press release later today. Congratulations."

I was quiet for a moment before my mind and voice found each other.

"Thank you for calling and please tell the governor I said thank you."

I was happy to be nominated for an appointment to the bench, but I was thrilled to be nominated to fill Judge Stout's vacancy. This seat came with history.

As soon as I hung up the telephone, Phyllis popped back into my office. "You got it, didn't you?" she asked, her eyes gleaming and a big smile on her face.

I nodded yes. We hugged and she asked who I wanted to call first. I had a few minutes before my next meeting. I called Michael, Dad, Julia, and Jimmie. They all congratulated me. Both Jimmie and Julia said the same thing: "Okay, now we got to get to work and prepare for the next steps." Finally, I called and left a message for the mayor.

In June 1988, I was confirmed by the Pennsylvania Senate. On July 15, 1988, I was sworn in publicly as a judge of the Commonwealth of Pennsylvania Court of Common Pleas, First Judicial District, Philadelphia, Pennsylvania. Almost everyone who supported and encouraged me, from the first time I told Dad that I wanted to be lawyer when I was six years old until this day, was there in person or in spirit.

Epilogue

I took my seat on the bench, again at an end that opened the door to another beginning. In 1989, I successfully ran in a citywide election for a 10-year term on the bench. I didn't know it at that time, but the lessons awaiting me on the bench were going to be an advanced course, not in the law, but in life, justice, and the quest for equal opportunity. With faith, hope, and confidence, I believe that the lessons that brought me this far prepared me for what was ahead.

Now I must run, not walk. There is work to do and much to be accomplished. When God chooses the unlikely, He makes all things possible.

My husband, Michael J. Lewis, our son, Michael Streeter

My family. My foundation. Many were seated in the jury box. Others arrived early to get a seat as close to the front as possible.

It was standing room only at the swearing in ceremony. Seated speakers: Left to right, Reverend Vaughn Wilson, Councilwoman Marian B. Tasco, Reverend Dr. Frank B. Mitchell.

I dreamed of becoming a lawyer. Now I wait to become a judge.

In attendance: Left to right, Honorable William F. Hall, Honorable Clifford Scott Green, Honorable Lawrence J. Prattis and Honorable Patreese Tucker.

Mayor W. Wilson Goode, first African American Mayor, Philadelphia, PA and one of my first employers, gives remarks.

State Senator Hardy Williams, who assisted me through the state senate confirmation process, gives remarks. Seated in the jury box on the front row, second from the left, is Mrs. Epsie Holmes, my fourth-grade teacher, who by example, taught me to reach beyond my job description.

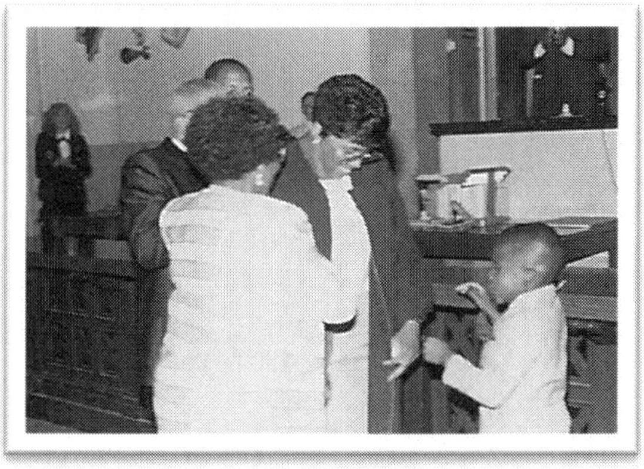

Mom, Dad (above), Michael and our son (below), help me into my robe as I assume my new role.

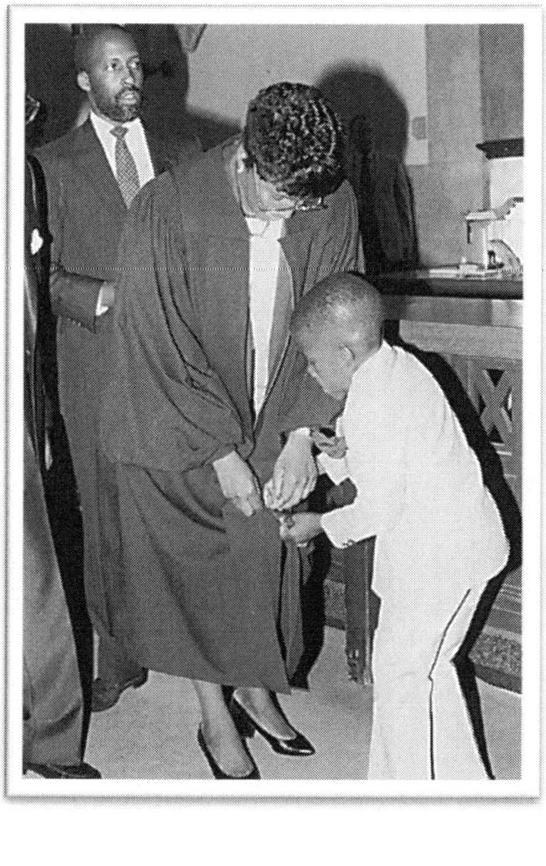

Presiding at the swearing in ceremony, left to right: Honorable A. Leon Higginbotham, Jr., U.S. 3rd Circuit Court of Appeals, Honorable Edward J. Bradley, President Judge Court of Common Pleas, Honorable Juanita Kidd Stout, Justice, Pennsylvania Supreme Court, Honorable Nicholas A. Cipriani, Administrative Judge Family Court Division.

It's official.
I take my seat on the bench.

I stand with my mentor, role model, and judicial colleagues.

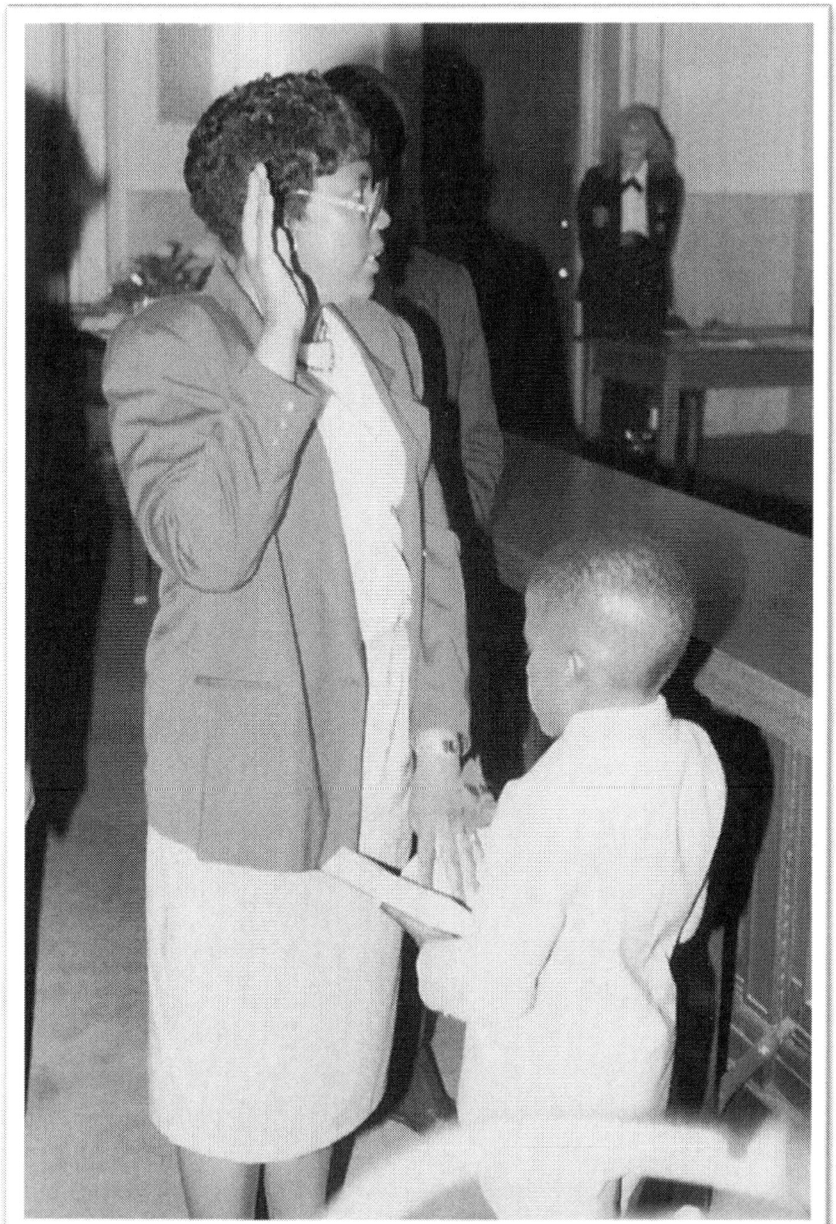

I take the Oath of Office as Michael holds the Bible.
July 15, 1988.

Acknowledgements

Getting my memoir, *When The Unlikely Are Chosen*, to what I proclaimed to be the finish line was one of the most arduous tasks I have ever undertaken. Unlike duties assigned to me as a student, teacher, lawyer, judge, commissioner or administrator, the task to write about the journey depicted in these pages was difficult. It was painful to pull scabs off of wounds, some of which I never revealed to anyone. This memoir was my chance to say thank you to so many people who gave of themselves to help me achieve my goal. It also reminded me of my responsibility to follow their positive examples. I dare not even try to name everyone who touched my life and helped me, for fear that I leave anyone out. From the bottom of my heart, I thank every one of you.

There are some people who would not let me just talk about writing my story. They were always ready to help move the process forward. I am forever grateful to my beta readers. These are the people who, with knowledge, insight, and care, read every draft manuscript as it transcended from one story to another and expanded over the years. They always insisted that I remain true to my voice and feelings. Because they know me so well and have watched this process from its beginning, they knew when I strayed from the story I wanted to tell and reminded me to evaluate all critiques through the lens of the warrior who came through the battles and not just someone who wanted to write a book. They never gave up on me and they didn't let me give up or make excuses why I couldn't finish this task. Aubra Spaulding Gaston, Esquire,

Marilyn Coates Bradley and Michael Streeter Lewis were my beta readers and unrelenting cheerleaders. The process of writing this book reaffirms that God sends angels to help me finish any task He assigns to me.

I also want to thank Mrs. Phyllis Mass, the instructor and visionary of Write Now—a creative writing workshop in Philadelphia that I had the good fortune to venture into several years ago. Phyllis guided each participant in the workshop through in-depth critiques of our writing projects. In an effort to make our writing better, she expected critiques to be constructive and considerate. I won't name everyone in the workshop who critiqued chapters, but I thank all of you. I also extend gratitude to Catresa Meyers, Esquire who provided literary services that brought the finish line, components required for publication, into view. As an attorney, published author, playwright, her insight, knowledge and experience were invaluable.

Acknowledgements are inadequate to express the depth of my gratitude and love to my family, beginning with my mother, Margaret Streeter, who encouraged me to write my story. In every endeavor I pursued in life, her support was steadfast and unconditional. I regret that I didn't get this book published before she transitioned in 2017. Next, my husband, Michael, urged me to make the writing experience a priority after I retired from the bench. Our son Michael was not only a beta reader but a marketing consultant and my transitional career strategist. My family never let me forget that my story reflected a portion of our family's legacy that needed to be preserved.

ABOUT THE AUTHOR

In the Summer 1989 edition of *Barrister*, the Young Lawyers Division of the American Bar Association published an article titled, "Charged with Excellence: 20 Young Attorneys Whose Work Stands Out." Judge Kathryn Streeter Lewis was one of the attorneys featured in that article, which stated:

> These lawyers represent the very highest quality of our profession. Their careers, their thoughts, should challenge each of us to be better lawyers, more active citizens and more compassionate people in general. They make a difference in our profession and in our world. They are 'supercharged' with excellence! Their challenge to each of us is to reach for the stars and to be the best that we can possibly be.

Judge Lewis retired after more than 20 years as a trial judge in Philadelphia, Pennsylvania. She has dedicated her career to public service and has received numerous awards and recognitions. She continues to serve on community and professional boards of directors.

When The Unlikely Are Chosen reveals Judge Lewis' path growing up in North Philadelphia, an impoverished tough neighborhood, graduating from Simon Gratz High School, a neighborhood public school, before attending the University of Pennsylvania and Villanova University School of Law. She was moved to write this memoir after she became a judge and began to question what made her path different from those brought before her in court. Further, her personal and professional experiences attest to the hurdles that women, especially black women, encounter as they pursue goals beyond what the status quo prescribed for them. Judge Lewis tells how she emerged with knowledge, strength, gratitude and joy.

Made in the USA
Middletown, DE
09 January 2020

82310318R00117